T0154753

Disney
PRINCESS
Baking

weldon**owen**

Contents

Chapter 2: Pies & Tarts

Chapter 3: Cakes & Cupcakes

Chapter 4: Morning Treats

Introduction

For over eighty years, since Snow White first appeared on the big screen, the princesses of Disney have captured the attention of the world, motivating us to achieve our dreams while staying true to ourselves. From the compassion and empathy of Snow White and the resourcefulness and optimism of Cinderella to the gentle grace of Aurora, Disney has instilled in its fans an inspirational vision of what it means to display the very best of who we are.

But just as empathy, optimism, and gentility are not emblematic of a particular gender or population, these traits do not fully define a Disney princess. With the second era of princess movies—dubbed the Disney Renaissance by fans—came a legion of princesses that changed the very idea of what being a princess meant. Ariel's free-spirited and confident demeanor, Belle's curiosity and assertiveness, Jasmine's adventurous and feisty nature, Pocahontas's nobility and open-mindedness, Mulan's tenacious independence— these women did not contradict the old notion of what it meant to be a princess. Instead, they expanded the vision to include both the traits for which we strive and those that are present in us.

Now, with the second Disney Renaissance underway, we're seeing the culmination of almost a century's worth of work. All of us—children and adults—have the hardworking and intelligent Tiana, the energetic and creative Rapunzel, and the defiant, take-charge Merida to remind us that although we cannot always achieve perfection, we can always strive for our own version of perfection—a perfection based on our true selves. That's what being a Disney princess is all about.

The drive to realize the best in ourselves is something to celebrate. However you wish to mark such magical moments—a birthday, a holiday, a graduation—a sweet treat is a good way to commemorate the occasion. Plus, baking for friends and family creates a lifetime of rewarding experiences.

No special occasion? No problem. With a little hard work and some Disney magic, you can take your destiny—and your desserts—into your own hands. Kick up your heels and have a Cinderella-style ball with a batch of Stroke-of-Midnight Moon Pies. Steal your friends for a Sunday-morning brunch with loaves of Aladdin Stolen Sweet Bread. Or grab your dinglehoppers and dive into a movie night with Ariel's Secret Grotto Cake. For all occasions big and small, life deserves a celebration. And when it comes to bringing a little Disney magic into your life, the only limits are your imagination.

Top-Notch Tips for Baking Like a Princess

Whether you're new to baking or a home-grown pro, it's always a good idea to brush up on the basics. Here are some helpful pointers for practicing kitchen safety while you're baking—as well as troubleshooting tips to achieve the best results with your magical baked goods.

STAY SAFE!

The best bakers know that safety is the most important thing when it comes to creating yummy treats. Here's what to know before rolling up your sleeves:

- Always ask an adult for help when you have questions or need assistance, especially when using the stove top, oven, and kitchen appliances, and whenever you need to use a knife or other sharp tools.

- Be extra careful with sharp knives and tools.

- Wash your hands with warm soapy water before cooking or handling ingredients.

- Remember to tie back your hair if it's long to keep it out of the way.

- Always stay in the kitchen if you have something on the stove top or in the oven. It's a good idea to set a timer so you don't forget to check if your dish is ready.

- Use thick, dry oven mitts when handling anything that is hot in order to protect your hands from burns. (Wet mitts or towels will burn!)

- Let hot pans cool before moving them to the sink or washing them.

- While it's tempting to sample baked goodies hot from the oven, don't forget to follow any cooling instructions in the recipe.

LEARN FROM THE MISTAKES!

If you encounter any baking issues, here are some common ways to troubleshoot and fix them. Whatever the issue, prevent food waste by getting creative! Crush overbaked cookies and sprinkle the crumbs atop ice cream. Turn fallen cakes into trifles. Transform pies with charred crusts into parfaits, layering the filling with whipped cream in glasses and crumbling the good bits of the crust on top.

Cookies

The cookies spread too much during baking: The butter was too soft when added, or the dough wasn't chilled long enough or was placed on a hot cookie sheet.

The cookies are burned on the bottom: The cookies were too thin, the oven was too hot, the cookie sheet was too thin or placed too low in the oven, or the pan was not rotated during baking.

The cookies did not bake evenly: The cookie sheet was not rotated during baking or the oven has hot spots.

Cakes

The top of the cake is overbrowned: If caught in time, loosely drape aluminum foil over the top of the cake as it finishes baking. If not, use a long serrated knife to trim off the overbrowned area.

The cake did not rise: The leavening agent was forgotten or was out of date and/or the oven was not hot enough. Use an oven thermometer to determine the oven's accuracy.

The cake is dry: The cake was overbaked or the batter was overbeaten. Unless otherwise directed, stop beating when the ingredients are evenly blended.

Pies

The pie fell apart when it was cut: Fruit pies just out of the oven are very juicy, so they must be left to cool completely before cutting to allow the juices to set up. Custard pies need time in the refrigerator to set properly.

The piecrust isn't flaky or is tough: The pie dough was too warm when rolling, the butter was warm when cut into the dry ingredients, the water added to the dough wasn't chilled, the butter and dough were overworked, and/or the dough wasn't chilled before baking.

The bottom crust is soggy: The oven temperature was too low, the oven rack was too high and the crust did not get enough heat, or the pie was not cooled on a wire rack, preventing air from circulating under it.

The edges of the pie are overbrowning: Cut strips of aluminum foil and crimp them over the edges of the crust as the pie finishes baking.

CHAPTER 1

Cookies & Bars

The Fairy Godmother's Magic Wand Marshmallow Krispies

Cinderella's Fairy Godmother represents hope, and her wand has the magical power to transform an everyday object into something spectacular. These edible star-shaped wands, made from crisp rice cereal, will enchant party guests. Choose your favorite colored ribbons and colored sprinkles to match your party theme and let the magic happen!

3 tablespoons unsalted butter

4 cups miniature marshmallows

6 cups crisp rice cereal, such as Rice Krispies

All-purpose flour for dusting

12 oz white chocolate chips (2 cups)

4 tablespoons solid vegetable shortening

Sprinkles for decorating

Makes about 12 pops

Recipe Twist

Substitute a handful of your favorite chopped nuts for the sprinkles.

Line the bottom of a 9 x 13-inch baking pan with parchment paper. Cut a second sheet of parchment paper the same size. Line a rimmed baking sheet with parchment paper.

In a large saucepan over low heat, melt the butter. Add the marshmallows and stir until completely melted. Add 3 cups of the cereal and stir until fully incorporated, being careful not to crush the cereal. Add the remaining 3 cups and stir until fully incorporated, again being careful not to crush the cereal. Remove from heat and let cool for 2 minutes.

Dump the cereal mixture into the prepared 9 x 13-inch pan. Lay the second sheet of parchment on top and, using your hands, gently press the cereal mixture until it is evenly distributed in the pan. Dust a 3½-inch-wide star-shaped cookie cutter with flour and cut out as many star shapes as possible, setting them aside on the parchment-lined baking sheet. Horizontally insert a wooden ice pop stick halfway into each star, leaving the other half exposed for using as a handle. Gather up the scraps and, working quickly before the mixture cools, press the scraps into the star-shaped cutter to make more pops. Insert ice pop sticks into the remaining pops. You should have a total of 12 pops.

In a small microwave-safe bowl, combine the chocolate chips and vegetable shortening and microwave for 25 seconds, then stir and continue to microwave, stopping to stir every 15 seconds, just until melted and smooth.

Pour the sprinkles into a small bowl. Carefully dip each pop into the melted chocolate, swirling the pop to coat evenly, and then dip into the sprinkles to coat. Return the pops to the parchment-lined baking sheet. Refrigerate for 20 minutes to set the chocolate before serving. The pops can be stored in an airtight container for up to 3 days.

Jasmine Pistachio Honey Baklava

Popular throughout much of the Middle East, baklava is a honey-laced dessert made of toasted nuts spread between layers of crisp, buttery filo dough. It is often reserved for special occasions—like Jasmine and Aladdin's engagement—and is typically prepared with walnuts or pistachios or a combination of the two. Be sure to begin to thaw your filo dough in the refrigerator the day before you plan to bake. You will need only 10 to 12 ounces of the filo; reserve the rest for another use.

1 lb roasted pistachios, plus ¼ cup finely ground pistachios for garnish (optional)

¼ cup sugar

1 teaspoon ground cinnamon

¾ cup (1 ½ sticks) unsalted butter

1 lb package frozen filo dough, thawed according to package directions

For the Honey Syrup

1 cup sugar

¾ cup honey

¾ cup water

1 cinnamon stick

1 orange peel strip

Makes 24 pieces

Preheat the oven to 350°F.

In a food processor, combine the 1 lb pistachios, sugar, and cinnamon and process until the nuts are finely ground but still have some texture (do not process to a fine meal). Divide the mixture evenly among 4 small bowls.

In a small saucepan over low heat, melt the butter. Remove from the heat and brush a 9 x 13-inch pan with some of the butter.

Unroll the thawed filo sheets and lay them on a clean, flat work surface. Using a sharp knife, trim the stack of sheets to fit the prepared pan. Cover the filo stack with a sheet of plastic wrap and then a lightly dampened towel to prevent it from drying out, always re-covering the stack after removing a sheet. (If you use only the towel, the filo could get wet and stick together.) Remove a filo sheet from the stack, lay it on the bottom of the pan, and brush it lightly but thoroughly with butter. Top with a second filo sheet and brush it with butter. Continue to layer and butter sheets until you have a total of 7 sheets in the pan. (If the butter begins to cool, place it over low heat to make sure it stays melted and slightly warm.)

Spread one-fourth of the pistachio mixture evenly over the filo. Repeat to layer 5 more filo sheets the same way, brushing each sheet with butter. Gently spread another one-fourth of the pistachio mixture over the filo. Repeat this two more times, layering and buttering 5 filo sheets and topping with one fourth of the nut mixture. Top the final addition of nut mixture with 7 layers of buttered filo. Brush the top sheet with butter.

Using a large, sharp knife, cut the layered filo into 12 squares, then cut each square into a triangle, for 24 pieces total. Bake the baklava until crisp and golden brown, about 40 minutes.

While the baklava bakes, make the honey syrup. In a small saucepan, stir together the sugar, honey, water, cinnamon stick, and orange peel. Bring to a boil over medium-high heat, then reduce the heat to low and simmer, stirring occasionally, until the mixture has a slightly syrupy consistency, about 15 minutes. Remove from the heat and let cool to room temperature.

When the baklava is ready, transfer the pan to a wire rack. Remove the cinnamon stick and orange peel from the syrup. Slowly and evenly pour the syrup over the baklava, getting it into all the nooks and crannies. Set aside at room temperature for at least 4 hours or up to overnight.

To serve, garnish with the ground pistachios, if desired. The baklava can be covered and stored at room temperature or in the refrigerator for up to 2 weeks.

Ariel Under-the-Sea Shells

These vanilla-scented treats, known as madeleines, are more like mini sponge cakes than cookies. They are baked in traditional shell-shaped molds and then dipped in a sea of white chocolate, creating a seashell sweet fit for a princess (or mermaid).

4 tablespoons (½ stick) unsalted butter, melted and cooled, plus more for the pan

½ cup all-purpose flour, plus more for the pan

2 large eggs

⅓ cup sugar

¼ teaspoon salt

1 teaspoon pure vanilla extract

⅓ cup white chocolate chips

Makes 12 madeleines

Recipe Twist

Forgo the chocolate dip in favor of a lighter strawberry-lemon topping: Combine ⅓ cup mashed strawberries, 1 tbsp fresh lemon juice, a pinch of confectioners' sugar and ¼ tsp honey, whisk with a fork, and spread atop the madeleines.

Preheat the oven to 375°F. Using a pastry brush, coat the 12 molds of a madeleine pan with melted butter, being careful to coat every ridge and flute. Dust the molds with flour, tilting and shaking the pan to coat the surfaces evenly, then tap out the excess.

In a large bowl, using an electric mixer, beat together the eggs, sugar, and salt on medium-high speed until light and fluffy, about 5 minutes. Add the vanilla and beat until blended. Turn off the mixer and scrape down the bowl with a rubber spatula. Sift the flour over the egg mixture. Beat on low speed just until the flour is incorporated. Turn off the mixer. Using a rubber spatula, gently fold in half of the melted butter just until blended. Then gently fold in the remaining melted butter.

Scoop a heaping tablespoon of the batter into each mold. Bake the madeleines until the tops spring back when lightly touched, 10–12 minutes. Invert the pan onto a wire rack and tap the pan on the rack to release the madeleines. If any of them stick, use a butter knife to loosen the edges, then invert and tap again. Let cool completely.

To dip the madeleines in chocolate, line a rimmed baking sheet with parchment paper. Put the chocolate chips in a small microwave-safe bowl and microwave, stopping to stir every 20 seconds, just until melted and smooth. Do not overheat the chocolate or it will seize (become thick and lumpy). One at a time, dip the wide, rounded end of each madeleine into the chocolate, then set the madeleine, fluted side up, on the prepared pan.

Refrigerate the madeleines until the chocolate is set, 10–15 minutes, then serve. They are best eaten the same day they are baked.

Aurora Magical Kiss Cookies

When Maleficent curses Aurora at birth with death on her sixteenth birthday, the three good fairies—Flora, Fauna, and Merryweather—soften the spell with an enchanted sleep that can be broken only by a kiss from Aurora's true love. These chewy peanut butter cookies, with a kiss of chocolate crowning the middle, are a great choice for a *Sleeping Beauty* movie night.

1¼ cups creamy peanut butter, at room temperature

²/₃ cup firmly packed light brown sugar

1 large egg

1 teaspoon pure vanilla extract

½ cup all-purpose flour

About 25 chocolate kiss candies, unwrapped

Makes about 25 cookies

Preheat the oven to 350°F. Line a cookie sheet with parchment paper.

In a large bowl, using an electric mixer, beat together the peanut butter and sugar on medium speed until smooth and creamy, about 30 seconds. Turn off the mixer and scrape down the bowl with a rubber spatula. Add the egg and vanilla and beat on medium speed until blended. Reduce the speed to low, add the flour, and beat just until combined.

Scoop up a rounded tablespoonful of dough and roll it between your palms into a ball. Place the ball on the prepared cookie sheet. Repeat with the remaining dough, spacing the balls about 1 inch apart.

Bake the cookies until they puff and appear dry on top, 10–12 minutes. Transfer the pan to a wire rack. Immediately place a chocolate candy, tip pointing up, in the center of each cookie and press down gently to sink its base into the cookie. Let the cookies cool on the pan for 10 minutes, then transfer them to the rack and let cool completely before serving. Leftover cookies will keep in an airtight container at room temperature for up to seven days.

Rapunzel Sundrop Flower Cookies

A single drop of sunlight falls through the heavens to create these magical golden flowers, which have the power to heal and to prevent aging. The flowers are the source of Rapunzel's incredibly long, magical hair and enable the villainous Mother Gothel to retain her youth. Eating these lemon-glazed gingerbread cookies may not help you grow tower-length hair or stay young forever, but they are heavenly.

For the Cookies

2½ cups all-purpose flour, plus more for the work surface

2 teaspoons ground ginger

½ teaspoon ground cinnamon

½ teaspoon baking soda

½ teaspoon salt

¼ teaspoon ground nutmeg

½ cup (1 stick) unsalted butter, at room temperature

¼ cup granulated sugar

¼ cup firmly packed light brown sugar

1 large egg

½ cup unsulphured molasses (not blackstrap)

For the Icing

1½ cups confectioners' sugar

About 3 tablespoons fresh lemon juice

A few drops yellow food coloring (optional)

Purple, orange, or white nonpareils for decorating

Makes about 18 cookies

To make the cookies, in a medium bowl, mix together the flour, ginger, cinnamon, baking soda, salt, and nutmeg. In a large bowl, using an electric mixer, beat together the butter and granulated and brown sugars on medium speed until light and fluffy, about 2 minutes. Add the egg and beat until blended, about 1 minute. Reduce the speed to low and gradually beat in the molasses until blended. Turn off the mixer and scrape down the bowl with a rubber spatula. Add the flour mixture and beat on low speed until combined, about 30 seconds.

Dump the dough onto a work surface and press into a mound. Divide the dough in half and press each half into a thick disk. Wrap each disk in plastic wrap and refrigerate for at least 1 hour or up to 2 days.

Line 2 cookie sheets with parchment paper. Place 1 dough disk on a lightly floured work surface and roll out into a round about ¼ inch thick. Using a 4-inch flower-shaped cookie cutter, cut out as many flowers as possible. Transfer the cutouts to a prepared cookie sheet, spacing them at least 1 inch apart. Gather up the dough scraps, press them together, wrap in plastic wrap, and refrigerate. Repeat with the second chilled dough disk. Then combine the scraps from both disks, press them into a disk, and roll out and cut out more flowers. If the dough becomes too warm to work with, wrap and refrigerate for 10 minutes before rerolling. Refrigerate the cutout cookies while you preheat the oven.

Position 2 oven racks in the middle of the oven and preheat to 375°F. Bake the cookies, rotating the pans between the racks halfway through baking, until lightly browned on the bottom, 8–10 minutes. Let cool on the pans on wire racks for 5 minutes, then transfer the cookies to the racks and let cool completely.

To make the icing, sift the powdered sugar into a bowl, then whisk in the lemon juice until completely smooth. Divide the icing equally into small bowls, one for each color being used. In one bowl, whisk a few drops of yellow food coloring. In the other bowls, whisk a few drops of the other preferred colors. Add more lemon juice to the icings if needed to create a thick but spreadable consistency.

Using a small offset or icing spatula, spread the yellow icing in a thin layer over the top of each cookie. Spoon the other colored icings into separate pastry bags, each fitted with a small round tip. Pipe a ring of one color and a ring of another color icing on top of the yellow icing. Using a toothpick and starting at the center of the flower, drag a thin line of icing towards the end of each petal. Sprinkle a pinch of nonpareils, if using, onto the center of each cookie while the icing is still wet, then let stand until the icing is set, about 20 minutes, before serving. The cookies will keep in an airtight container in a single layer or in multiple layers separated by parchment at room temperature for up to 3 days.

Moana Heart of Te Fiti Pinwheels

The Heart of Te Fiti is an ancient stone with the ability of creation. More than a millennium after it was stolen and then lost, Moana is chosen by the ocean to return the heart to its rightful place on the mother island of Te Fiti, thus restoring the balance of nature. These yummy green spiral cookies, which can be flavored with just vanilla or given a peppermint accent, were inspired by the swirly decorative Heart of Te Fiti.

2 cups all-purpose flour

1 teaspoon baking powder

¼ teaspoon salt

¾ cup (1½ sticks) unsalted butter, at room temperature

¾ cup granulated sugar

1 large egg yolk

1½ teaspoons pure vanilla extract

¼ teaspoon plus ⅛ teaspoon green gel food coloring, plus more if needed

½ teaspoon pure peppermint extract (optional)

About ½ cup decorating sugar for rolling (optional)

Makes about 48 cookies

In a medium bowl, mix together the flour, baking powder, and salt. In a large bowl, beat together the butter and granulated sugar on medium speed until fluffy and pale, about 5 minutes. Turn off the mixer and scrape down the bowl with a rubber spatula. Add the egg yolk and vanilla and beat on medium speed until blended. Reduce the speed to low, add half the flour mixture, and beat just until combined. Add the remaining flour mixture and beat just until combined.

Dump the dough onto a clean work surface, press into a mound, and divide in half. Return half to the bowl and add the ¼ teaspoon green food coloring and the peppermint extract, if using. Knead gently until well combined and evenly colored. If you want the color darker, add more food coloring, a dab or two at a time, and gently knead it in. Put the remaining half of the dough into a clean bowl, add the remaining ⅛ teaspoon green food coloring, and knead gently until well combined and evenly colored, adjusting the color with more coloring if desired.

Cut 4 sheets of waxed paper, each one about 18 inches long. Set the darker green dough on the center of a sheet of waxed paper sheet and use your hands to shape the dough into a rough rectangle. Cover the darker dough with a second sheet of waxed paper sheet and, using a rolling pin, roll out the dough into a 16 x 10-inch rectangle. Repeat with the lighter green dough and the remaining 2 waxed paper sheets. Peel off the waxed paper from the top of each dough rectangle.

Using the waxed paper, pick up the lighter green rectangle and carefully flip it over onto the darker green rectangle, lining up the edges as evenly as possible. Using your hands, press down gently but firmly on the light green layer to seal the layers together. Slowly peel off the top layer of waxed paper. Leave the bottom layer in place. If needed, using a small knife, trim the edges so they match up evenly. Starting at a long side, carefully lift and curl the edge of the dough over. Then, using the waxed paper as an aid, tightly roll up the dough into a log, peeling away the paper as you go. Press gently against the seam to seal.

Continued on page 26

If desired, scatter the decorating sugar evenly on a rimmed baking sheet and roll the log in the sugar to coat the outside. Wrap the log tightly in plastic wrap and refrigerate until firm, at least 1 hour or up to overnight.

Position 2 oven racks in the middle of the oven and preheat to 350°F. Line 2 cookie sheets with parchment paper.

Unwrap the dough log and set it on a cutting board. Using a large knife, trim both ends so they are even. Then cut the log crosswise into ¼-inch-thick slices. Place the slices on the prepared cookie sheets, spacing them about 2 inches apart. Using a paring knife, cut dashes, carets, and diamonds into the cookie according to the pattern seen on the Heart of Te Fiti.

Bake the cookies, rotating the pans between the racks and rotating them back to front halfway through baking, until they are firm to the touch, about 12 minutes. Let cool on the pans on wire racks for 5 minutes, then transfer the cookies to the racks and let cool completely. The cookies will keep in an airtight container at room temperature for up to one week.

Recipe Twist

Whether you use vanilla or peppermint extract, these cookies pair well with fresh strawberries.

Pocahontas Harvest Bars

Celebrate the autumn harvest with these oat and dried fruit bars, sweetened naturally with dates and honey and flavored with nut butter and cinnamon. You can personalize the bars by using any kind of nut butter, including nut-free sunflower seed butter, and your own choice of dried fruit. Take the bars to princess level by drizzling them with melted white chocolate.

Nonstick cooking spray

2 cups old-fashioned rolled oats

1 cup crisp rice cereal, such as Rice Krispies

⅓ cup dried blueberries or cranberries or raisins

½ teaspoon salt

½ teaspoon ground cinnamon

½ cup packed chopped pitted dates (about 12 dates)

¼ cup honey

3 tablespoons almond, peanut, or sunflower seed butter

3 tablespoons coconut oil or avocado oil

Makes about 12 bars

Preheat the oven to 350°F. Lightly spray the bottom and sides of a 9-inch square baking pan with cooking spray. Line the bottom and two opposite sides with parchment paper, allowing it to extend past the rim by about 2 inches on both sides.

In a large bowl, mix together the oats, cereal, dried blueberries, salt, and cinnamon. In a food processor, combine the dates, honey, almond butter, and oil and process to a smooth purée, about 2 minutes. Add the date mixture to the oat mixture and stir until well combined. You might want to use your clean hands to mix everything—the mixture is really thick.

Scoop and scrape the granola mixture out into the prepared pan and press it firmly onto the bottom. Use a flat-bottomed glass to help create a well-packed, even layer. Bake until golden brown, about 20 minutes. Let cool in the pan on a wire rack just until cool enough to handle but still warm, about 15 minutes.

Holding the edges of the parchment like handles, lift the bar straight up and out of the pan and set on a cutting board. Carefully pull away the parchment. Using a large, sharp knife, cut in half crosswise, then cut each half into 6 equal bars. Remove the pan from the rack, then set the rack in the pan. Arrange the bars on the rack and let cool completely. The bars will keep in an airtight container at room temperature for up to 1 week.

Jasmine Magic Carpet Cookies

Shy but curious, Magic Carpet, better known as Carpet, joins Aladdin on his adventure to win the heart of Jasmine—saving Aladdin's life a few times along the way. These pistachio-semolina cookies, which are based on Middle Eastern *ghraybeh*, have a tender, crumbly texture similar to shortbread and are scented with cardamom, orange zest, and orange blossom water. Be sure to give your carpet cookies an eye-catching design with a pretty piece of lace or a paper doily.

¼ cup pistachios

1 cup all-purpose flour, plus more for the work surface

½ cup semolina flour

½ cup confectioners' sugar, plus more for dusting

½ teaspoon baking powder

¼ teaspoon ground cardamom or cinnamon

¼ teaspoon salt

10 tablespoons (1¼ sticks) unsalted butter, at room temperature, cut into cubes

Grated zest of 1 orange

1 large egg

1 tablespoon orange flower water

Makes 16 cookies

Recipe Twist

Boost the fiber and calcium content with a date spread: In a food processor, combine ½ cup pitted Medjool dates, 2 tbsp fresh orange juice, and a pinch of ground cinnamon and pulse until a thick paste forms. Slather the spread between two cookies and serve.

In food processor, pulse the pistachios to a fine meal. Add the all-purpose and semolina flours, sugar, baking powder, cardamom, and salt and process until evenly mixed. Scatter the butter and orange zest over the flour mixture and process until the mixture is evenly moistened and looks like bread crumbs. Add the egg and orange flower water and pulse until well combined. Add the flour mixture and pulse just until blended. Cover the dough and refrigerate until chilled, at least 30 minutes or up to overnight.

Preheat the oven to 350°F. Line 2 cookie sheets with parchment paper.

On a lightly floured work surface, roll out the dough into a rectangle just slightly larger than 16 by 8 inches and about ¼ inch thick. Trim the edges on all four sides to make them even. Cut the dough into 16 rectangles, each about 2 by 4 inches. Divide the rectangles evenly between the prepared pans, spacing them about 1 inch apart. Using a paring knife, make 6–8 evenly spaced cuts, each ½ inch long, along the two short sides of each dough rectangle to create "fringe."

One at a time, freeze the pans of cookies for 15 minutes before baking to help the cookies hold their shape. Place 1 cookie sheet of cookies into the oven and bake until the cookies are very lightly golden and look dry, about 15 minutes. Let cool on the pan on a wire rack for 10 minutes, then transfer the cookies to the rack and let cool completely. Repeat with the remaining cookie sheet of cookies.

Lay a clean piece of lace or a paper doily on top of the cookies. Using a fine-mesh sieve, dust with confectioners' sugar, creating a pretty carpet-like pattern on the cookies. Carefully lift away the lace or doily, then serve. Alternatively, just dust the tops with confectioners' sugar. These cookies are best eaten the same day they are baked.

Merida Raspberry Scottish Empire Biscuits

The iced buns that Merida's triplet brothers—Harris, Hubert, and Hamish—feast on at the dinner table are based on traditional Scottish empire biscuits. Like their namesakes, these shortbread sandwich cookies are filled with raspberry jam and topped with a simple vanilla icing. Try to keep your little brothers away from these irresistible treats or they'll all disappear!

For the Biscuits

¾ cup (1½ sticks) unsalted butter, at cool room temperature, cut into cubes

⅓ cup granulated sugar

½ teaspoon salt

1 large egg yolk

2 teaspoons pure vanilla extract

2 cups all-purpose flour, plus more for the parchment and dough

For the Icing

1 cup confectioners' sugar, sifted

1 tablespoon whole milk, plus more if needed

½ teaspoon pure vanilla extract

6 glacé cherries, halved, or about 1 tablespoon raspberry jam for topping

⅓ cup raspberry jam for filling

Makes 12 sandwich cookies

To make the biscuits, in a large bowl, using an electric mixer, beat together the butter, granulated sugar, and salt on medium-low speed until creamy, about 1 minute. Increase the speed to medium, add the egg yolk and vanilla, and beat until well combined, about 30 seconds. Turn off the mixer and scrape down the bowl with a rubber spatula. Add the flour and beat on low speed until fully incorporated and the dough starts to clump together, about 30 seconds. Turn off the mixer and scrape down the bowl with the spatula. Beat again on low speed for 10 seconds. Turn the dough out onto a work surface and press into a thick disk. Wrap in plastic wrap and refrigerate for at least 30 minutes or up to 1 day.

Position 2 oven racks in the middle of the oven and preheat to 350°F. Line 2 large rimmed baking sheets with parchment paper.

Lay a large piece of parchment paper on a work surface and dust lightly with flour. Place the dough on the floured parchment. If it feels too stiff to roll out easily, let it stand for a few minutes to soften slightly. Lightly dust the top of the dough with flour, then roll it out into a round about ¼ inch thick. If it starts to tear, press the edges back together. Using a 2½-inch round cookie cutter (fluted or plain), cut out as many rounds as possible. Divide the rounds evenly between the prepared pans, spacing them 1 inch apart. Gather up the dough scraps, press them together, roll out, and cut out more rounds. Divide them evenly between the prepared pans. You should have 24 rounds total.

Bake the cookies, rotating the pans between the racks and rotating them back to front halfway through baking, until golden brown on the edges, 13–16 minutes. Let cool completely on the pans on wire racks.

To make the icing, in a small bowl, whisk together the confectioners' sugar, milk, and vanilla until smooth. The icing should be thick but spreadable. If it is too thick, add milk, ½ teaspoon at a time, until it is spreadable.

Set aside half of the cookies. Using a small offset spatula or icing spatula, spread the top of the remaining cookies with the icing, dividing it evenly. Top each iced cookie with a cherry half, if using. If not using the cherries, top each cookie with a small dollop of jam once the icing has set; it's best to do this shortly before serving, as the jam will "bleed" into the icing. Set the iced cookies aside on the pan until the icing is set, about 30 minutes.

Turn the reserved cookies bottom side up. Spoon a scant 1½ teaspoons jam onto each cookie, then, using the clean offset or icing spatula, spread the jam in an even layer almost to the edge. Top the raspberry-spread cookies with the iced cookies. Serve right away.

Evangeline the Evening Star Cookies

Evangeline is a bright star in the sky beloved by Ray the lightning bug in *The Princess and the Frog*. Here she is transformed into star-shaped lemony butter cookies that will be beloved by anyone who eats them! Be sure the star cutouts are chilled when they go into the oven so they keep their shape during baking.

For the Cookies

2⅓ cups all-purpose flour, plus more for the work surface

¼ teaspoon baking powder

⅛ teaspoon salt

1 cup (2 sticks) unsalted butter, at room temperature

⅔ cup granulated sugar

1 large egg

1½ teaspoons pure vanilla extract

For the Icing

1 cup confectioners' sugar

4 teaspoons fresh lemon juice

2–3 dabs yellow gel food coloring

White nonpareils for decorating

Makes 12 cookies

Recipe Twist

Arrange these brilliant star cookies on a platter alongside a mix of blueberries, blackberries, and red grapes to create a starry night sky effect.

To make the cookies, in a medium bowl, mix together the flour, baking powder, and salt. In a large bowl, using an electric mixer, beat together the butter and sugar on medium speed until fluffy and pale, about 5 minutes. Turn off the mixer and scrape down the bowl with a rubber spatula. Add the egg and vanilla and beat on medium speed until blended. Add the flour mixture and beat on low speed just until combined. Turn off the mixer and scrape down the bowl with the spatula.

Dump the dough onto a clean work surface and press into a mound. Divide the dough in half, press each half into a thick disk, and wrap each disk in plastic wrap. Refrigerate until firm, at least 1 hour or up to overnight.

Position 2 oven racks in the middle of the oven and preheat to 350°F. Line 2 cookie sheets with parchment paper.

Place 1 dough disk on a lightly floured work surface and roll out into a round about ¼ inch thick. Using a 3½-inch star-shaped cookie cutter, cut out as many stars as possible. Transfer the cutouts to a prepared pan. Gather up the dough scraps, press them together, wrap in plastic wrap, and refrigerate. Repeat with the second chilled dough disk. Then combine the scraps from both disks, press them into a disk, and roll out and cut out more stars. If the dough becomes too warm to work with, wrap and refrigerate until firm. Refrigerate each pan of cookies as you finish filling it.

Bake the cookies, rotating the pans between the racks and rotating them back to front halfway through baking, until golden, 15–20 minutes. Let cool on the pans on wire racks for 10 minutes, then transfer the cookies to the racks and let cool completely.

To make the icing, sift the confectioners' sugar into a bowl, then whisk together the lemon juice and 2 dabs of the food coloring until smooth. If you want a deeper color, whisk in another dab of food coloring.

Using a small offset spatula or icing spatula, spread the icing on the tops of the cooled cookies. Alternatively, spoon the icing into a pastry bag fitted with a small tip and pipe it onto the top of each cookie, outlining the edge of the cookie first and then filling in the center. Decorate the cookies with the nonpareils while the icing is still wet, then let stand until the icing is set, about 20 minutes, before serving. The cookies will keep in an airtight container in a single layer or in multiple layers separated by parchment at room temperature for up to 7 days.

Rapunzel Oatmeal–Chocolate Chip Cookies

Being locked away in a tower leaves Rapunzel with plenty of time on her hands, so she likes to bake to stay busy. Her usual chocolate chip cookies are updated here with oats and spices. For a crunchier result, let them bake for a few minutes longer. And for a special treat, put a small scoop of ice cream between two cookies for an ice cream sandwich.

2 cups all-purpose flour

1 teaspoon baking powder

½ teaspoon baking soda

½ teaspoon salt

2 teaspoons ground cinnamon

¼ teaspoon ground nutmeg

1 cup (2 sticks) unsalted butter, at room temperature

¾ cup granulated sugar

¾ cup firmly packed light brown sugar

2 large eggs

1½ teaspoons pure vanilla extract

2½ cups old-fashioned rolled oats

2½ cups semisweet chocolate chips

Makes about 36 cookies

Position 2 oven racks in the middle of the oven and preheat to 375°F. Line 2 cookie sheets with parchment paper.

In a medium bowl, sift together the flour, baking powder, baking soda, salt, cinnamon, and nutmeg. In a large bowl, using an electric mixer, beat together the butter and granulated and brown sugars on medium speed until light and fluffy, about 3 minutes. Reduce the speed to low and add the eggs one at a time, beating well after each addition. Add the vanilla and beat until blended, about 1 minute. Turn off the mixer and scrape down the bowl with a rubber spatula. Add the flour mixture and beat on low speed until combined. Add the oats and chocolate chips and beat until combined. Turn off the mixer and scrape down the bowl with the spatula. Beat again on low speed for 10 seconds.

Drop the dough by rounded tablespoons onto the prepared cookie sheets, spacing them about 2 inches apart. Gently flatten each mound with your hand to about ½ inch thick. Bake the cookies, switching the sheets between the racks and rotating them back to front halfway through baking, until golden brown, 9–11 minutes. Let cool on the pans on wire racks for 3 minutes, then transfer the cookies to the racks and let cool for at least a few minutes before serving. Serve warm or at room temperature. Leftover cookies will keep in an airtight container at room temperature for up to 7 days.

Recipe Twist

To swap in natural sugars for refined, replace the chocolate chips with ½ cup chopped toasted walnuts.

Ariel Clamshell Macarons

Although Ariel is more enchanted by dinglehoppers and snarfblats than she is by pearls, these decorated "clamshell" macarons are sure to impress your two-legged guests (and possibly your seagull and fish friends, too). If the macarons test done to the touch but are still sticking to the parchment, pop them back into the oven for a few minutes longer.

2 cups confectioners' sugar, sifted

1⅓ cups almond flour (not almond meal)

3 large egg whites

1 teaspoon pure vanilla extract

½ teaspoon pure almond extract

¼ teaspoon cream of tartar

⅛ teaspoon salt

About ½ teaspoon blue or purple gel food coloring

White Chocolate Frosting (page 131)

12 white or blue sugar pearls

Edible white glitter or pearl dust for decorating (optional)

Makes 12 sandwich cookies

Line 2 large rimmed baking sheets with parchment paper. Using a scalloped shell about 1½ inches in diameter as a template, trace 24 shells on each parchment sheet, spacing them about 1 inch apart. (Alternatively, use a 1½-inch round cookie or biscuit cutter to trace 24 circles on each parchment sheet.) Turn the parchment over. The shell outlines will be visible through the paper. Combine 1 cup of the confectioners' sugar and the almond flour in a fine-mesh sieve. Set aside.

In a large bowl, using an electric mixer, beat together the egg whites, vanilla and almond extracts, cream of tartar, and salt on medium-high speed until foamy, about 30 seconds. Increase the speed to high and gradually beat in the remaining 1 cup confectioners' sugar, then continue beating until stiff, glossy peaks form, about 2 minutes longer.

Sift about one-third of the reserved confectioners' sugar–almond flour mixture over the beaten whites. Using a rubber spatula, fold in gently just until blended. Repeat to fold in the remaining confectioners' sugar mixture in two batches. Add the food coloring and continue to fold the mixture just until the ingredients are fully combined and the batter flows in a slow, thick ribbon (about 40 strokes).

Spoon the batter into a pastry bag fitted with ⅜-inch round tip. Holding the pastry bag with the tip about ½ inch above a prepared pan, and using the shell outlines on the parchment sheets as a guide, thickly pipe the batter onto pans. Pipe the outline first, exaggerating the scalloped top of the shell, and then fill in the middle. Tap each sheet firmly against the work surface two or three times to release any air bubbles. Let the cookies stand at room temperature until they look less wet and are a little tacky, 45–60 minutes.

Preheat the oven to 300°F. Place 1 sheet of cookies into the oven and bake until the cookies have risen and set but not browned, about 20 minutes. The bottoms of the cookies should be dry and firm to the touch and not stick to the parchment paper (if they stick, bake them a few minutes longer). Let cool on the pan on a wire rack for 1 minute, then transfer to the rack and let cool completely. Repeat with the remaining cookie sheet of cookies.

While the cookies bake, make the frosting.

Turn half of the cookies bottom side up. Spread about 1½ teaspoons of the frosting onto each cookie. Top with the remaining cookies, bottom side down, pressing the base together gently so the scalloped edge opens slightly like a shell.

Place the cookies in a single layer on a rimmed baking sheet, cover with plastic wrap, and refrigerate for at least 1 day or up to 3 days or freeze in an airtight container for up to 6 months. If freezing, once frozen, stack them in an airtight container, then thaw in the refrigerator before serving. Just before serving, add a sugar pearl to the middle outside scalloped edge of each shell and dust the top of the shell with edible glitter, if using. Serve chilled or at cool room temperature.

Merida Scottish Shortbread

A classic Scottish treat, buttery shortbread is thought to have evolved from medieval biscuit bread, which was made by turning leftover bread dough into twice-baked hard, dry biscuits dusted with sugar. In time, butter replaced the yeast in the dough, and biscuit bread became shortbread—a luxury in Merida's medieval Scotland. To update this recipe, add 1 tablespoon grated citrus zest to the dough with the vanilla.

1½ cups all-purpose flour, plus more for shaping the dough

¼ teaspoon salt

1 cup (2 sticks) unsalted butter, at room temperature

¼ cup confectioners' sugar

¼ cup plus 1 tablespoon granulated sugar

2 teaspoons pure vanilla extract

Makes 18 cookies

Preheat the oven to 300°F. Have ready a 9-inch square baking pan.

In a medium bowl, sift together the flour and salt. In large bowl, using an electric mixer, beat the butter on medium speed until fluffy and pale yellow, about 3 minutes. Add the confectioners' sugar and ¼ cup of the granulated sugar and continue beating until the mixture is no longer gritty when rubbed between your finger and thumb, 2–3 minutes. Add the vanilla and beat until blended. Turn off the mixer and scrape down the bowl with a rubber spatula. On low speed, gradually add the flour mixture, beating just until blended.

Transfer the dough to the baking pan and, using floured fingertips, press it evenly into the pan. Sprinkle the dough evenly with the remaining 1 tablespoon granulated sugar. Bake the shortbread until the edges are golden, about 1 hour.

Remove the pan from the oven and, using a thin, sharp knife, immediately cut the shortbread into rectangles about 1 by 3 inches. Prick the surface of each rectangle a few times with fork tines to create a decorative pattern. Let the rectangles cool in the pan on a wire rack for 30 minutes, then carefully transfer the rectangles to the rack and let cool completely. The cookies will keep in an airtight container at room temperature for up to seven days.

Recipe Twist

Accompany these deliciously crumbly shortbreads with a bowl of sliced nectarines and a tall, cold glass of milk.

Stroke-of-Midnight Moon Pies

At the stroke of midnight, the spell cast by the Fairy Godmother is broken and Cinderella must flee from the prince so her secret is not revealed. These gooey moon pies, made of homemade graham cookies sandwiched with marshmallow crème and dipped in dark-as-night chocolate, take time to put together but are worth it. And unlike Cinderella, you don't want them to get away!

For the Cookies

1 cup finely ground graham cracker crumbs (about 6 full-size crackers)

1 cup all-purpose flour, plus more for the work surface

½ teaspoon baking powder

½ teaspoon ground cinnamon

½ teaspoon salt

½ cup (1 stick) unsalted butter, at room temperature

½ cup firmly packed dark brown sugar

1 large egg

1 teaspoon pure vanilla extract

2 tablespoons whole milk

About 1¾ cups marshmallow crème

For the Chocolate Coating

2⅔ cups (1 lb) semisweet chocolate chips

2 tablespoons vegetable oil

Makes about 15 sandwich cookies

Recipe Twist

Switch up this classic combination of marshmallow, chocolate, and graham crackers by swapping out the marshmallow crème for protein-packed peanut butter.

To make the cookies, in a medium bowl, mix together the graham cracker crumbs, flour, baking powder, cinnamon, and salt. In a large bowl, using an electric mixer, beat together the butter and sugar on medium-high speed until light and fluffy, about 1 minute. Add the egg and vanilla and beat until blended. Turn off the mixer and scrape down the bowl with a rubber spatula. Add the graham cracker mixture and beat on low speed until combined. Add the milk and beat just until the dough comes together. Transfer the dough to a clean work surface and press into a thick disk. Wrap the disk in plastic wrap, and refrigerate for at least 1 hour or up to overnight.

Preheat the oven to 350°F. Line 2 large rimmed baking sheets with parchment paper. On a lightly floured surface, roll out the dough into a round about ⅛ inch thick. Using a fluted 2¾-inch round or crescent-shaped cookie cutter, cut out as many cookies as possible. Transfer them to the prepared pans, spacing them at least 1 inch apart. Gather up the dough scraps, press them together, roll out, and cut out more cookies. Add them to the pans. You should have about 30 cookies.

Place 1 baking sheet of cookies into the oven and bake the cookies until lightly golden around the edges, about 13 minutes. Transfer the cookies to a wire rack and let cool completely. Repeat with the remaining baking sheet of cookies.

Turn half of the cookies bottom side up. Dollop about 2 tablespoons marshmallow crème onto the center of each overturned cookie. Top with a second cookie, bottom side down, and press the top cookie gently so the crème fills the sandwich. Place the filled cookies on a rimmed baking sheet, cover with plastic wrap, and place in the freezer to firm up, at least 20 minutes or up to overnight.

To make the coating, in a small saucepan, pour water to a depth of about 1 inch and bring to a gentle simmer over medium-low heat. Put the chocolate chips into a heatproof bowl that will rest on the rim of the pan. Place the bowl on the saucepan over (not touching) the water. Heat, stirring occasionally, until the chocolate melts and is smooth. Remove from the heat and let cool slightly, then stir in the oil. Let cool for about 5 minutes.

To coat the cookies, place a wire rack on a rimmed baking sheet. Immerse a chilled filled cookie into the melted chocolate and use 2 forks to maneuver it so it is evenly coated. Transfer to the wire rack. Repeat with the remaining cookies. Refrigerate the cookies until the chocolate hardens, at least 30 minutes. Serve chilled or at room temperature. The cookies will keep in an airtight container in the refrigerator for up to 5 days.

Rajah the Tiger Icebox Cookies

These adorable tiger cookies capture the love of Rajah, Princess Jasmine's loyal pet tiger and constant companion. His regal name comes from stories Jasmine's mother told her at a young age about a star called Rajah. These vanilla-and-chocolate-striped butter cookies are easier to make than they look, plus you can prepare the dough a day in advance of baking.

2 cups all-purpose flour, plus more for the work surface

½ teaspoon baking powder

¼ teaspoon salt

½ cup (1 stick) unsalted butter, at room temperature

⅔ cup granulated sugar

1 large egg

1 teaspoon pure vanilla extract

¼ teaspoon orange gel food coloring

¼ cup unsweetened natural cocoa powder

1 large egg beaten with 1 teaspoon water for brushing

Royal Icing (page 130)

¼ teaspoon black gel food coloring

Makes about 24 cookies

In a medium bowl, mix together 1¾ cups of the flour, the baking powder, and salt. In a large bowl, using an electric mixer, beat together the butter and granulated sugar on medium speed until light and fluffy, about 3 minutes. Add egg and vanilla and beat until blended. Turn off the mixer and scrape down the bowl with a rubber spatula. On low speed, gradually add the flour mixture, beating just until blended and stopping to scrape down the bowl if needed.

With the dough still in the bowl, press it into a mound and then divide it in half. Transfer half of the dough to a clean bowl. Add the remaining ¼ cup flour and the orange food coloring to the dough in the original bowl and beat on low speed until the flour and coloring are fully incorporated and the dough is evenly colored. Press the dough into a thick disk, wrap in plastic wrap, and refrigerate. Return the remaining dough to the large bowl. Add the cocoa and beat on low speed until fully incorporated and the dough is evenly colored. Press the dough into a thick disk, wrap in plastic wrap, and refrigerate. Refrigerate both disks for at least 30 minutes or up to overnight.

Remove the dough disks from the refrigerator. If the dough disks have been refrigerated for 1 hour or longer, let them sit at room temperature for about 30 minutes before rolling to soften until pliable. Line a rimmed baking sheet with parchment paper.

Cut off 2 oz of the dough from the orange disk. Cut the piece in half. On a clean work surface, shape half into a stubby log. Then, using the palms of your hands, roll the dough back and forth against the surface, starting at the middle and gently working outward until you have a rope 11 inches long. Using your fingertips, pinch the top of the rope along its length to form a triangle-shaped rope. Repeat with the other half of the dough. Transfer both ropes to the prepared pan.

Continued on page 40

Rajah the Tiger Icebox Cookies *continued from page 39*

Have ready a large sheet of parchment paper. Roll out the rest of the orange disk into an 8 x 6-inch rectangle. Then roll out the cocoa disk into an 8 x 6-inch rectangle. If needed, using a small knife, trim the edges so they are even and the rectangles measure exactly 8 by 6 inches. Cut each rectangle lengthwise into 4 equal pieces; each piece will be 1½ inches wide and 8 inches long. Brush the top of each piece lightly with the egg wash. Stack the dough pieces, alternating the colors. Transfer the stacked dough to the parchment paper and, using your hands, rock the dough back and forth to blunt the edges and create a round-edged log about 11 inches long. Transfer the log to the baking sheet with the ropes and refrigerate for 10 minutes.

Brush the top of the log with the egg mixture, then lay the 2 triangular ropes on the top (these will be the ears of the tiger), pressing gently so they adhere. Refrigerate for 20 minutes.

Position 2 oven racks in the middle of the oven and preheat to 350°F. Line a second rimmed baking sheet with parchment paper. Unwrap the dough log and set it on a cutting board. Using a large knife, trim both ends so they are even. Then cut the log crosswise into ¼-inch-thick slices. Place the slices on the prepared baking sheets, spacing them about 2 inches apart.

Bake the cookies, switching them between the racks and rotating them back to front halfway through baking, until the edges are lightly browned, 12–14 minutes. Let cool on the pans on wire racks for 10 minutes, then transfer the cookies to the racks and let cool completely.

Make the royal icing as directed. Divide the icing into two small bowls. Stir the black food coloring into one bowl of icing, and leave the other half white. Spoon the white icing into a pastry bag fitted with a small round tip. Spoon the black icing into a second pastry bag fitted with a small round tip. To decorate each cookie, using the white icing, pipe 2 rounds for the eyes, 2 rounds for the muzzle, and 2 small triangles for the inner ears. Let stand for 15 minutes to set. Using the black icing, pipe 1 dot to finish each eye, pipe a nose and mouth, and pipe 3 dots to finish each muzzle round. Let stand until the icing sets, about 30 minutes, before serving. The cookies will keep in an airtight container at room temperature for up to 7 days.

Briar Rose Meringues

For sixteen years, Princess Aurora was affectionately known as Briar Rose by the three good fairy aunts who raised her in the forest to protect her from an evil curse. These gluten-free lighter-than-air meringues can be tinted pink or red or any hue in between. Piping the stiffly beaten egg whites into a tight, thick spiral creates a beautiful meringue rose. Flavor these special treats with vanilla or, to make them extra rosy, use rose water instead.

3 large egg whites, at room temperature

¼ teaspoon cream of tartar

⅛ teaspoon salt

¾ cup sugar

2 teaspoons pure vanilla extract or ½ teaspoon pure rose extract

Red or pink gel food coloring

For the Chocolate Dip (Optional)

⅔ cup semisweet chocolate chips

2 teaspoons coconut oil or solid vegetable shortening

Makes about 15 meringues

Recipe Twist

For a creamy, fruity addition rich in calcium and potassium, crumble these meringues over a bowl of Greek yogurt and top with fresh berries.

Position 2 oven racks in the middle of the oven and preheat to 250°F. Line 2 large rimmed baking sheets with parchment paper. Using a 3-inch round cookie or biscuit cutter or overturned water glass, trace 8 circles on each parchment sheet, spacing them about 2 inches apart. Turn the parchment over. The circles will be visible through the paper.

In a large bowl, using an electric mixer, beat together the egg whites, cream of tartar, and salt on medium-high speed until foamy, about 30 seconds. Add the sugar, 1 tablespoon at a time, and beat until incorporated. Turn off the mixer and scrape down the bowl with a rubber spatula. On medium-high speed, continue to beat the mixture until it is thick and glossy and holds stiff peaks, about 4 minutes. Add the vanilla and enough food coloring to achieve the color you desire and beat until the meringue is evenly colored, about 1 minute.

Spoon the meringue into a pastry bag fitted with a large star tip. For each rose, pipe a dot of meringue onto the center of a circle on the parchment, building it about ½ inch high. Then pipe rings of the meringue around the dot, keeping the rings tight and close together to build up the height of the rose, until you reach the edge of the circle. You should have about 15 meringues.

Bake the meringues until they feel firm and dry, 1–1¼ hours. Turn off the oven, crack the door with the handle of a wooden spoon, and let the meringues remain in the oven for 1 hour to cool slowly. Then transfer the pans to wire racks.

If you want to dip the cookies in chocolate, in a small microwave-safe bowl, combine the chocolate chips and coconut oil. Microwave for 25 seconds, then stir and continue to microwave, stopping to stir every 15 seconds, just until melted and smooth. Dip the underside of a meringue into the melted chocolate, then, using a small offset spatula, spread the chocolate over the bottom to fill in any gaps. Scrape off the excess against the side of the bowl and return the meringue to the baking sheet. Repeat with the remaining meringues. Let stand until the chocolate sets, about 30 minutes. The meringues can be stored in an airtight container at room temperature for up to 3 days.

Lucky Cri-kee Almond Cookies

Cri-kee, the endearing "lucky" cricket who acts as Mushu's sidekick in *Mulan*, is both eager to please and effective. His luck shines time and time again through his resilience. Make and eat these Chinese almond butter cookies and you'll be lucky too! Press a whole blanched or natural almond into the center of each cookie before baking, and don't skip the egg wash. It gives each cookie a beautiful shine.

½ cup (1 stick) unsalted butter, at room temperature

½ cup sugar

¼ teaspoon salt

1 large egg

½ teaspoon pure almond extract

1 cup all-purpose flour

½ teaspoon baking soda

½ cup almond flour

1 large egg beaten with 1 teaspoon water for brushing

18–20 whole almonds

Makes 18–20 cookies

In a large bowl, using an electric mixer, beat together the butter, sugar, and salt on medium speed until pale and fluffy, about 2 minutes. Add the egg and almond extract and beat until blended. Turn off the mixer and scrape down the bowl with a rubber spatula. Sift together the flour and baking soda over the butter mixture, then add the almond flour. Beat on low speed just until combined. Press the dough into a ball, cover the bowl, and refrigerate for at least 1 hour or up to overnight.

Preheat the oven to 325°F. Line a large rimmed baking sheet with parchment paper.

Scoop up a tablespoon of the dough and roll it between your palms into a ball about 1 inch in diameter. Place on the prepared pan. Repeat with the remaining dough, spacing the balls about 1½ inches apart. You should have 18–20 balls. Using your hand, flatten each ball to about ¼ inch thick. The cookies should be at least 1 inch apart. Place a whole almond in the center of each cookie. Brush each cookie lightly with the egg mixture.

Bake the cookies until golden, about 20 minutes. Transfer the cookies to a wire rack and let cool completely. The cookies are best eaten the day they are baked, but they can be stored in an airtight container at room temperature for up to 1 week (they will soften slightly).

Recipe Twist

If your leftover cookies have softened, make cookie sandwiches! Add a pinch of ground cinnamon to vanilla-flavored Greek yogurt, spread liberally on the bottom of a cookie, top with a second cookie, bottom side down, and enjoy immediately.

CHAPTER 2

Pies & Tarts

Percy the Pug's Cherry Streusel Tart

Percy, the spoiled pug of Governor Ratcliffe in *Pocahontas*, loves eating cherries—especially while taking a bubble bath! When sly, food-loving Meeko the raccoon, Pocahontas's companion, unexpectedly shows up in the tub, he eats all of Percy's cherries. Percy and Meeko would probably love to get their hands on this delicious cherry tart topped with crunchy-sweet streusel. You can use frozen cherries, canned sour cherries, or jarred dark Morello cherries for the filling, with each lending its own character and tart-sweet level. If you opt for sour cherries, increase the sugar to ⅔ cup.

Tart Pastry (page 129)
Nonstick cooking spray

For the Streusel

¾ cup all-purpose flour

⅓ cup sugar

Pinch of salt

5 tablespoons unsalted butter, melted

1 teaspoon pure vanilla extract

For the Filling

4 cups drained jarred Morello or other dark cherries (about two 24-oz jars)

½ cup sugar

3 tablespoons tapioca starch or cornstarch

Makes 8 serving

Recipe Twist

To increase the fiber and add crunch, add ½ cup chopped toasted almonds, pecans, or walnuts to the streusel along with the melted butter.

Make and refrigerate the pastry dough as directed.

Lightly spray a 9-inch tart pan with a removable bottom with cooking spray. On a lightly floured work surface, roll out the dough into a round 12 to 13 inches in diameter and about ⅛ inch thick. If the dough tears, press it back together. Roll the dough loosely around the rolling pin and unroll it over the prepared tart pan. Gently press the dough onto the bottom and up the sides of the pan. Using kitchen scissors or a small knife, trim the edge of the dough, leaving a 1-inch overhang. Fold the overhang down inside the pan and press against the sides to reinforce them. Refrigerate for at least 15 minutes or up to overnight.

Preheat the oven to 375°F. To make the streusel, in a bowl, combine the flour, sugar, and salt and stir together with a fork. Add the butter and vanilla and stir until the mixture is evenly moistened and crumbly.

To make the filling, in a bowl, combine the cherries, sugar, and tapioca starch and toss to mix evenly. Pour the filling into the chilled tart shell. Top with the streusel, spreading it evenly.

Place the tart pan on a rimmed baking sheet. Bake the tart until the filling is bubbly and the streusel and crust are golden brown, about 1 hour. Let cool on the baking sheet on a wire rack for at least 30 minutes before serving. To unmold, set the tart pan on an overturned bowl and gently slide the tart ring downward. Then, using a wide offset spatula, carefully move the tart from the pan bottom to a serving plate. The tart can be served warm, at room temperature, or chilled.

Tiana Fruit-Filled Praline Cups

Southern pecan praline is an old-fashioned sweet made with brown sugar, butter, and toasted pecans. It is a common sight in candy shops all over New Orleans, where *The Princess and the Frog* is set. This variation transforms pecan praline into cup-shaped bowls for holding fresh fruit and whipped cream. You can use any ripe, in-season fresh fruit you love.

½ cup (1 stick) unsalted butter, plus more room-temperature butter for the foil and cups

1 cup granulated sugar

1 cup all-purpose flour

½ cup finely chopped almonds or pecans

½ cup light corn syrup

⅔ cup firmly packed dark brown sugar

Sliced fresh fruit, such as peaches, plums, or figs for serving

Whipped cream (page 131) for serving (optional)

Makes 12 praline cups

Recipe Twist

Greek yogurt is an excellent substitution for whipped cream for this Southern-inspired treat.

Preheat the oven to 375°F. Cut aluminum foil into twelve 8-inch squares and butter one side of each square. Place 2 foil squares, buttered side up, on a rimmed baking sheet, spacing them at least 2½ inches apart. Butter the outside bottom and sides of 2 custard cups or flat-bottomed ½-cup measuring cups.

In a bowl, mix together the granulated sugar, flour, and nuts. In a small saucepan over medium-high heat, combine the ½ cup of butter, corn syrup, and brown sugar and bring to a gentle boil, stirring constantly. Stir in the flour-nut mixture, mixing well, and then remove from the heat. Drop 2 rounded tablespoons of the mixture onto the center of each foil square on the baking sheet.

Bake the praline until it bubbles and spreads out into 4- to 5-inch rounds, about 7 minutes. Remove from the oven and let cool on the baking sheet for 2 minutes. Place 1 buttered custard cup or measuring cup in the center of each praline circle. Holding the cup in place, lift up the foil and gently mold the praline to the outside of the cup.

Cool upside down for 3 minutes, then carefully remove the custard cups. Turn the cups over onto a wire rack and let cool completely, then remove the foil. While the praline cups are cooling, repeat with the remaining praline mixture, buttering the cups again as necessary. If the praline mixture in the saucepan hardens, reheat gently over low heat just until softened.

To serve, fill the cooled praline cups with fruit and top with whipped cream, if desired.

Rapunzel Chocolate Hazelnut Tart

According to Mother Gothel, hazelnut soup is one of Rapunzel's favorite meals. But even that can't lift Rapunzel's spirits when she realizes that she's been forced to live in a tower against her will and that Mother Gothel isn't even her real mother. Although the soup did not help Rapunzel, this double-chocolate hazelnut tart promises to lift your spirits. The cocoa-hazelnut dough can be made a day in advance.

For the Crust

Nonstick cooking spray

1 cup all-purpose flour

½ cup ground hazelnuts

⅓ cup unsweetened natural cocoa powder

¼ cup sugar

¼ teaspoon salt

½ cup (1 stick) cold unsalted butter, cut into cubes

¼ cup whole milk, plus more if needed

1 teaspoon pure vanilla extract

For the Filling

3 tablespoons unsalted butter

2 oz unsweetened chocolate, chopped

3 large eggs

1 cup light corn syrup

½ cup sugar

1 teaspoon pure vanilla extract

¼ teaspoon salt

1½ cups hazelnuts, toasted and skinned, then coarsely chopped

Makes 6–8 servings

To make the crust, lightly spray a 9-inch tart pan with a removable bottom with cooking spray.

In a food processor, combine the flour, hazelnuts, cocoa, sugar, and salt. Scatter the butter over the flour mixture and pulse for a few seconds until the butter is slightly broken up into the flour. Add the milk and vanilla and process just until evenly moistened and the mixture starts to come together. If the dough seems too dry, add more milk, 1 teaspoon at a time, pulsing once or twice after each addition, as needed. Dump the dough into the prepared pan. Using your hands, press and pat the dough evenly over the bottom and up the sides of the pan. Refrigerate until ready to use.

Preheat the oven to 425°F. To make the filling, fill a small saucepan with water to a depth of about 1 inch, place over low heat, and bring to a bare simmer. Put the butter and chocolate into a small heatproof bowl that will fit snugly on the rim of the pan and set over (not touching) the simmering water. Heat, stirring occasionally, until the mixture is melted and smooth. Remove from the heat and let cool slightly.

In a bowl, whisk the eggs until blended. Add the corn syrup, sugar, vanilla, and salt and whisk until the sugar dissolves and all the ingredients are fully incorporated. Add the chocolate mixture and whisk until combined. Add the hazelnuts and stir until evenly distributed.

Pour the filling into the tart crust. Bake for 15 minutes. Reduce the oven temperature to 350°F and continue to bake until the filling is set around the edges and the center jiggles slightly when the pan is gently shaken, about 25 minutes. Let cool completely in the pan on a wire rack. To unmold, set the pan on an overturned bowl and gently slide the tart ring downward. Then, using a wide offset spatula, carefully move the tart from the pan bottom to a serving plate. Serve at room temperature.

Belle "Be Our Guest" Tartlets

These elegant chocolate-raspberry mini tarts would entice anyone to want to be your guest! In *Beauty and the Beast*, the castle's staff of enchanted objects—plates and pots, cutlery and candlesticks—tries to welcome Belle with a festive multicourse musical feast. You can make the tart dough and line the pans well in advance, then bake and fill the pastry shells just before serving them at your own feast.

For the Dough

½ cup (1 stick) unsalted butter, at cool room temperature, cut into pieces

⅓ cup confectioners' sugar, sifted

1 large egg yolk

1 teaspoon pure vanilla extract

¼ teaspoon salt

1¼ cups all-purpose flour

¼ cup unsweetened natural cocoa powder

Nonstick cooking spray

For the Filling

1 cup heavy cream

2 tablespoons seedless raspberry jam

12 fresh raspberries for garnish

Confectioners' sugar for dusting

Makes 12 tartlets

Recipe Twist

The light, airy whipped filling provides a nice contrast to the dense chocolate pastry shells. But these shells are also good packed with banana slices, berries, or other fruit.

To make the dough, in a large bowl, using an electric mixer, beat together the butter, confectioners' sugar, egg yolk, vanilla, and salt on medium-low speed until smooth and creamy, about 1 minute. Turn off the mixer and scrape down the bowl with a rubber spatula. Sift together the flour and cocoa powder over the butter mixture and beat on low speed just until the mixture is evenly moistened and starts to clump together, about 1 minute. Dump the dough onto a clean work surface and press into a thick disk. Wrap the disk in plastic wrap and refrigerate for at least 30 minutes or up to overnight.

Lightly spray 12 standard muffin cups with cooking spray. On a lightly floured work surface, roll out the dough into a round about ⅛ inch thick. If the dough tears, press it back together. Using a 3¼-inch fluted cookie cutter, cut out as many rounds as possible. Gather up the scraps, press them together, roll out, and cut out more rounds as needed to total 12 rounds. Transfer each round to a prepared muffin cup, gently pressing it evenly onto the bottom and partly up the sides. Place the lined muffin cups in the freezer to firm up for 30 minutes before baking.

Preheat the oven to 350°F. Bake the tartlet shells until cooked through, about 15 minutes.

Let cool in the cups on a wire rack for 10 minutes, then carefully remove the tartlet shells from the muffin cups and let cool completely on the rack.

When the shells are cool, make the filling. In a bowl, using an electric mixer, beat together the cream and raspberry jam on medium-high speed until stiff peaks form, about 5 minutes. The peaks should stand straight when the beaters are lifted. Be careful not to overwhip.

Spoon the filling into a pastry bag fitted with a large star tip. Pipe the cream into the tartlet shells, dividing it evenly. Top each tartlet with a raspberry. Using a fine-mesh sieve, dust the tops with confectioners' sugar. Serve right away.

Spinning Wheel Tart

As a baby, Princess Aurora is cursed by Maleficent to prick her finger on a spinning wheel's spindle before the sun sets on her sixteenth birthday, sending her into a deep sleep (originally the fate was death, but the good fairy Merryweather was able to lighten the curse). Despite the kingdom's effort to protect her, Aurora touches the spindle and activates the curse, leaving her with the nickname Sleeping Beauty. This creamy vanilla bean custard tart uses fragrant fresh mango slices and tart-sweet raspberries to recreate the wheel.

Tart Pastry (page 129)
Nonstick cooking spray

For the Custard
1 vanilla bean
1½ cups whole milk
4 large egg yolks
½ cup sugar
2 tablespoons cornstarch
2 tablespoons unsalted butter

1 ripe mango for decorating
9 fresh raspberries for decorating

Makes 8 servings

Make and refrigerate the pastry dough as directed.

Lightly spray a 9-inch tart pan with a removable bottom with cooking spray. On a lightly floured work surface, roll out the dough into a round 12 to 13 inches in diameter and about ⅛ inch thick. If the dough tears, press it back together. Roll the dough loosely around the rolling pin and unroll it over the prepared tart pan. Gently press the dough onto the bottom and up the sides of the pan. Using kitchen scissors or a small knife, trim the edge of the dough, leaving a 1-inch overhang. Fold the overhang down inside the pan and press against the sides to reinforce them. Refrigerate for at least 15 minutes or up to overnight.

Preheat the oven to 375°F. Line the tart shell with parchment paper and fill with pie weights. Bake the tart shell until it looks dry, about 15 minutes. Remove from the oven, then remove the weights and parchment. Return the tart shell to the oven and bake until golden brown, about 10 minutes longer. Let cool on a wire rack.

While the tart shell bakes, make the custard. Using a paring knife, split the vanilla bean lengthwise, then use the back of the knife to scrape out the seeds. In a saucepan over medium heat, combine the milk and the vanilla bean pod and seeds and heat just until the milk starts to steam; do not allow it to boil. Remove from the heat. In a bowl, whisk together the egg yolks, sugar, and cornstarch until the sugar and cornstarch dissolve and the mixture is smooth. Remove the vanilla bean pod from the hot milk. Slowly add about 1 cup of the hot milk mixture to the egg yolk mixture while whisking constantly. Then pour the combined mixtures back into the saucepan while whisking constantly.

Return the saucepan to medium-low heat and cook, stirring constantly with the whisk, until the mixture thickens, about 4 minutes. Add the butter and stir with the whisk until melted, then remove from the heat. Pour the custard through a fine-mesh sieve into the cooled tart shell, spreading it evenly. Cover with a piece of plastic wrap, pressing it directly onto the surface (to prevent a "skin" from forming). Refrigerate until cold and set, about 2 hours.

To decorate the tart, stand the mango on one of its narrow sides on a cutting board. Using a large, sharp knife, cut just slightly to one side of the center (you want to cut as close to the pit as possible), slicing downward to remove the flesh from the large, flat pit. Rotate the mango 180 degrees and cut the flesh away from the pit on the opposite side the same way. Using a large metal spoon, scoop the flesh away from the peel from both pieces and discard the peel. Slice the mango flesh lengthwise into ¼-inch-thick strips. (Slice the flesh off both edges of the pit, cut away the peel, and enjoy the flesh as a baker's treat!)

Set aside 8 mango strips. Arrange the remaining strips around the outer edge of the tart, overlapping them slightly, to create the rim of the wheel. Trim the 8 reserved strips as needed to form ½-inch-wide "spokes" that will reach from the center to the rim of the tart. Lay the strips on top of the tart, spacing them evenly to make the spokes of the wheel. Decorate with the raspberries, placing 1 berry in the center where the spokes meet and 1 berry on the end of each spoke. Refrigerate until ready to serve.

Snow White's Wishing Well Pie

Forced to be a scullery maid in the Evil Queen's castle, Snow White sings a sweet melody into the wishing well. Her song captivates the prince as he rides by the castle, charming him into the courtyard to join her in singing. The top of this blueberry-ginger pie is decorated with a twisted coil of dough that recalls the ripples in the depths of the wishing well. Omit the ginger for a classic blueberry pie.

Double-Crust Flaky Pie Dough (page 129)

4 pints fresh or thawed frozen blueberries (about 8 cups)

1 cup granulated sugar

1 tablespoon fresh lemon juice

1 teaspoon peeled and finely grated fresh ginger

Pinch of salt

¼ cup cornstarch

2 tablespoons unsalted butter, cut into small pieces

1 large egg beaten with 1 teaspoon water

Turbinado sugar for sprinkling

Makes 8–10 servings

Make and refrigerate the pie dough as directed.

Remove 1 dough disk from the refrigerator. On a lightly floured work surface, roll out the dough into a round about 13 inches in diameter and ⅛ inch thick. Roll the dough loosely around the rolling pin and unroll it over a 9-inch deep-dish pie dish. Gently press the dough onto the bottom and up the sides of the dish. Using kitchen scissors or a small knife, trim the edge of the dough, leaving a ½-inch overhang. Fold the dough under itself to create an edge on the rim of the dish. To make a decorative edge, flute the dough with your index finger and thumb or crimp with fork tines. Refrigerate the piecrust for 30 minutes.

Meanwhile, in a large saucepan over medium heat, combine the blueberries, granulated sugar, lemon juice, ginger, and salt and cook, stirring occasionally, until some of the berries begin to burst and the liquid reduces slightly, 5–7 minutes. Remove from the heat and fold in the cornstarch, mixing evenly. Let cool to room temperature. Preheat the oven to 350°F.

Clean the work surface and dust again with flour. Remove the second dough disk from the refrigerator and roll it out on the floured surface into a rectangle about 6 by 18 inches. Cut the rectangle lengthwise into six 1-inch-wide strips. Remove the piecrust from the refrigerator, pour in the cooled filling, and dot with the butter. Carefully twist 1 strip of dough, making the twists 1 inch apart. Starting at the center of the pie, gently lay the twisted dough strip in a coil. Pinch the end of a second strip to the first to seal, then twist and coil the second strip around the first. Continue to add and twist the remaining dough strips the same way, creating a continuous twisted coil over the entire pie filling. Brush the edge of the crust and the coiled strips with the egg mixture and sprinkle with turbinado sugar.

Place the pie dish on a rimmed baking sheet. Bake the pie until the crust is golden brown and the filling is bubbling, 50–55 minutes, covering the top and edges with aluminum foil if they begin to brown too quickly. Let cool on a wire rack for at least 4 hours or preferably overnight before serving.

Snow White Sleeping-Apple Pies

Tricked by the Evil Queen disguised as an elderly woman, Snow White bites into a bewitched apple and falls into a sleep-like coma—a spell that can only be broken by a kiss from her true love. These individual pies are so delicious—and so cute—that you can't help but fall in love with them. Make sure to cut the apples into uniform slices so they bake evenly.

Double-Crust Flaky Pie Dough (page 129)

¼ cup granulated sugar

¼ cup water

2 lb tart-sweet baking apples, such as Gala, Pink Lady, or Honeycrisp, peeled, cored, and cut into ⅛-inch-thick slices

1 teaspoon ground cinnamon

¼ teaspoon ground nutmeg

¼ teaspoon salt

Grated zest and juice of 1 lemon

1 large egg beaten with 1 teaspoon water

Turbinado sugar for sprinkling

Vanilla ice cream for serving

Makes 10 mini pies

Recipe Twist

Try these pretty little pies with a dollop of Greek yogurt in place of the ice cream.

Make and refrigerate the pie dough as directed.

On a lightly floured work surface, roll out 1 dough disk into a round about ⅛ inch thick. Using a 4-inch round pastry or cookie cutter, cut out as many rounds as possible. Transfer the rounds to a rimmed baking sheet. Gather up the dough scraps and set aside. Repeat with the remaining dough disk and add the rounds to the baking sheet. Gather up all the dough scraps, press them together, roll out, and cut out more rounds as needed to total 20 rounds. If you have extra dough, cut out 10 leaves and shape any remaining dough into small logs to use as stems. Transfer the leaves and stems to the baking sheet. Cover with plastic wrap and refrigerate until ready to make the pies. Let stand at room temperature for about 10 minutes before assembling the pies.

In a large sauté pan over medium heat, combine the granulated sugar and water and cook, stirring, until the sugar dissolves. Add the apples, cinnamon, nutmeg, and salt and cook, stirring occasionally, until the apples are just tender and the liquid is slightly thickened, 6–8 minutes. Transfer to a bowl and stir in the lemon zest and juice. Let cool to room temperature.

Meanwhile, preheat the oven to 400°F. Line 2 rimmed baking sheets with parchment paper.

Arrange 10 dough rounds on the prepared pans, spacing them at least 1 inch apart. Brush the rounds with a little of the egg mixture, then place about ¼ cup of the apple filling in the center of each round. Lay a dough round over each apple-topped round, press the top and bottom edges together, and then crimp the edges with fork tines. Brush the top of each pie with the egg mixture. If you have made stems and leaves, crimp the top and bottom of each pie so it looks more like the shape of an apple, then gently press a stem and a leaf onto the top edge of each pie. Cut small steam vents in the top of each pie. Sprinkle the pies lightly with turbinado sugar.

Refrigerate one sheet of pies and bake the other sheet of pies until the crust is golden brown, 18–22 minutes. Let cool on the pan on a wire rack for at least 15 minutes. Repeat with the remaining pies. Serve warm or at room temperature with a scoop of vanilla ice cream. The pies can be stored in an airtight container at room temperature for up to 7 days.

Cinderella
Maple-Pumpkin Pie

Cinderella didn't have a ride to the ball until her Fairy Godmother enchanted a big pumpkin, turning it into a magical carriage. Just as the pumpkin coach carried Cinderella in style, this delectable pumpkin pie will bring style to your table. The pie is flavored with a homemade mix of fragrant spices, but you can substitute 1½ teaspoons pumpkin pie spice for the mixture if you like.

Single-Crust Flaky Pie Dough (page 129)

1 can (15 oz) pumpkin purée (about 1½ cups)

⅔ cup firmly packed light brown sugar

½ cup pure maple syrup

¾ cup whole milk

½ cup heavy cream

2 large eggs, lightly beaten

2 tablespoons all-purpose flour

1 teaspoon ground cinnamon

¼ teaspoon ground ginger

⅛ teaspoon ground nutmeg

¼ teaspoon salt

Whipped Cream (page 131) for serving

Makes 8 servings

Make and refrigerate the pie dough as directed.

On a lightly floured work surface, roll out the dough into a round about 13 inches in diameter and ⅛ inch thick. Roll the dough loosely around the rolling pin and unroll it over a 9-inch deep-dish pie dish. Gently press the dough onto the bottom and up the sides of the dish. Using kitchen scissors or a small knife, trim the edge of the dough, leaving a ½-inch overhang. Fold the dough under itself to create an edge on the rim of the dish. To make a decorative edge, flute the dough with your index finger and thumb or crimp with fork tines. Chill in the freezer for about 20 minutes.

Preheat the oven to 400°F. Line the piecrust with parchment paper and fill with pie weights. Bake the crust until it starts to look dry, about 15 minutes. Remove from the oven, then remove the weights and parchment. Return the crust to the oven and bake until just barely golden, about 5 minutes. Let cool on a wire rack. Reduce the oven temperature to 350°F.

In a large bowl, whisk together the pumpkin, brown sugar, and maple syrup. Add the milk, cream, and eggs and whisk until well mixed. Sift together the flour, cinnamon, ginger, nutmeg, and salt over the pumpkin mixture, then whisk until fully incorporated.

Place the pie dish on a rimmed baking sheet. Pour the pumpkin mixture into the crust. Bake the pie until the filling is just set but still jiggles very slightly in the center when the pie dish is gently shaken, about 60–70 minutes. Let cool on a wire rack for at least 1 hour before serving. Accompany each serving with a big spoonful of whipped cream.

Enchanted Rose Pies

By rejecting an enchanted rose, the prince is transformed into a beast in *Beauty and the Beast*. But after he learns that beauty comes from within and earns Belle's love before the last petal drops from the rose, the spell is broken and he is restored to human form. For these mini pies, thin slices of tart-sweet apple are rolled into elegant roses fit for a prince! Be sure to mix the apple slices gently, or you'll end up with broken petals.

Single-Crust Flaky Pie Dough (page 129), prepared and refrigerated as directed

Nonstick cooking spray

4 large crisp-tart baking apples (about 2 lb total), such as Honeycrisp, Gala, or Pink Lady

3 tablespoons fresh lemon juice

2 tablespoons unsalted butter

½ cup firmly packed light brown sugar

¼ cup seedless raspberry jam

Makes 12 mini pies

Lightly spray 12 standard muffin cups with cooking spray. On a lightly floured work surface, roll out the dough into a round about ⅛ inch thick. Using a 4-inch round cookie cutter, cut out as many rounds as possible. Gather up the dough scraps, press them together, roll out, and cut out more rounds. You should have 12 rounds total. Transfer each round to a muffin cup, gently pressing the dough evenly onto the bottom and up the sides of the cup. The edge of the dough should reach just underneath rim of the cup. Place the lined muffin cups in the refrigerator while you prepare the apples.

Stand an apple, stem end up, on a cutting board. Using a sharp knife, and placing it just to the side of the stem, cut straight down. Rotate the apple 180 degrees and cut down the same way on the opposite side. Cut off the remaining 2 sides the same way and discard the core. You should have 4 pieces total, 2 large and 2 small. Trim the top and bottom off of the 2 large pieces. Using the same sharp knife or a mandoline, cut the larger pieces crosswise into very thin half-moons (about ¹⁄₁₆ inch). Cut the smaller apple pieces lengthwise into very thin half-moons. Transfer all the slices to a large bowl. Repeat with the remaining apples. Sprinkle the apple slices with the lemon juice and toss gently to coat evenly.

In a small saucepan over medium-low heat, melt the butter. Add the sugar and jam and, stirring constantly, bring to a gentle boil, about 2 minutes. Remove from the heat, pour over the apple slices, and stir gently to coat evenly, being careful not to break the slices. Transfer about one-third of the apples to a microwave-safe plate, spread in an even layer, and microwave for 1 minute to make them pliable. Transfer to a large rimmed baking sheet. Repeat with the remaining apples in two batches. Spread the apples in an even layer on the baking sheet.

Preheat the oven to 375°F. To make each apple rose, arrange about 12 apple slices, end to end, in a straight line, with each slice overlapping about halfway. The line of apple slices should be about 12 inches long. Starting at the end at which you laid down the first apple slice, gently roll up the apple slices, doing your best to keep the bottom aligned. Carefully transfer the apple "rose" to the center of a pastry-lined muffin cup. Fill in around the edges of the rose with additional slices. Repeat with the remaining apple slices to fill all the lined muffin cups.

Bake the pies until the crust is golden brown and the apples are tender, about 40 minutes. Let cool in the cups on a wire rack for at least 20 minutes before removing the pies from the cups. Serve warm or at room temperature.

Rapunzel Braided Mixed Berry Pie

When Rapunzel steals into town after escaping the tower, she has her hair braided and decorated with flowers by four young girls to keep it up and out of the way. This lattice-top berry pie is just as stunning as Rapunzel's elaborate braid, with braided strands woven with flat strips to create a work of pie art.

Double-Crust Flaky Pie Dough (page 129)

4 pints mixed fresh berries (about 8 cups), such as blackberries, blueberries, raspberries, and/or boysenberries

1 cup firmly packed light brown sugar

¼ cup cornstarch

Pinch of kosher salt

1 teaspoon grated lemon zest

2 tablespoons fresh lemon juice

1 large egg beaten with 1 teaspoon water

Turbinado sugar for sprinkling

Makes 8 servings

Make and refrigerate the pie dough as directed. Preheat the oven to 350°F.

On a lightly floured work surface, roll out 1 dough disk into a 12-inch round about ⅛ inch thick. Loosely roll the dough onto the rolling pin, then unroll it over a 9-inch pie dish. Gently press the dough into the bottom and up the sides of the dish. Using kitchen scissors or a small knife, trim the edge, leaving a 1-inch overhang. Refrigerate the lined pie dish.

Put the berries into a large bowl. Scatter the brown sugar, cornstarch, salt, and lemon zest and juice over the top and stir and toss gently until evenly mixed. Set aside.

Clean and dust the work surface with flour. Roll out the second dough disk into an oval about 15 inches long, 12 inches wide, and ⅛ inch thick. Cut the oval crosswise into at least 12 equal strips each about 1 inch wide and 12 inches long. Select 3 or more of the longer strips for creating braids and reserve 9 strips for the lattice top. For each braid, cut 1 strip lengthwise into 3 equal strips. Press the top ends together and, keeping the strips flat, braid them, then pinch the bottom ends together. Repeat to make 2 (or more) braids.

Continued on page 66

Rapunzel Braided Mixed Berry Pie continued from page 65

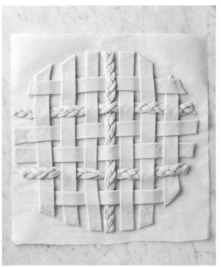  

Fill the lined pie dish with the berry mixture. Arrange the dough strips and the braids in a lattice on top of the berry filling: Lay half of the strips and braids over the pie parallel to each other, spacing them evenly apart. Fold back every other strip or braid halfway and lay down a strip or braid perpendicular across the unfolded strips and braids, then unfold the strips and braids back in place. Fold back the alternate strips or braids and repeat to lay down a strip or braid perpendicular across the unfolded strips and braids, then unfold the strips and braids back in place. Repeat with the remaining strips and braids to finish the lattice. Trim the edge of each strip or braid, leaving a 1-inch overhang.

Tuck the overhang of the bottom crust and the lattice under itself to create an edge on the rim of the dish. To make a decorative edge, flute the dough with your index finger and thumb or crimp with fork tines. Brush the lattice top and edge with the egg mixture. Sprinkle turbinado sugar all over the top of the pie.

Place the pie dish on a rimmed baking sheet. Bake the pie until the crust is golden brown and the filling is bubbling, 1–1¼ hours, covering the lattice and edge with aluminum foil if they begin to brown too quickly. Let cool on a wire rack for at least 4 hours or preferably overnight before serving.

Mulan Egg Custard Tartlets

Mulan is based on the Chinese legend of Hua Mulan, a female warrior who disguised herself to take the place of her aging father in battle. Mildly sweet and with a silky texture, Chinese-style egg custard tartlets were introduced in Macau and Hong Kong by Europeans but can be found throughout much of China today. A cream cheese dough is used here, but if you are short of time, a good-quality store-bought pie dough can be substituted.

For the Dough

1¼ cups all-purpose flour, plus more for the work surface

2 tablespoons sugar

¼ teaspoon salt

6 tablespoons (¾ stick) unsalted butter, at room temperature

3 tablespoons cold cream cheese

2 tablespoons ice-cold water

For the Filling

⅓ cup whole milk

2 tablespoons water

2 large eggs plus 1 egg yolk

⅓ cup sugar

Pinch of salt

1 teaspoon fresh lemon juice

½ teaspoon pure vanilla extract

Makes 12 tartlets

To make the dough, in a medium bowl, mix together the flour, sugar, and salt. In a large bowl, using an electric mixer, beat together the butter and cream cheese on medium speed until blended, about 1 minute. Add the flour mixture and water and beat on low speed until the dough forms large clumps. Turn off the mixer and scrape down the bowl with a rubber spatula.

Have ready 12 tartlet pans, each 3 inches in diameter and 1–1½ inches deep, and a rimmed baking sheet. Dump out the dough onto a lightly floured work surface. Press it into a rough log, then, using the palms of your hands, roll it back and forth until you have a fairly even log about 12 inches long. Cut the log crosswise into 12 equal pieces. Transfer each dough piece to a tartlet pan, gently pressing it evenly onto the bottom and up the sides of the pan. Place the lined pans on the baking sheet, cover, and refrigerate until the dough is cold and firm, at least 1 hour or up to overnight.

Preheat the oven to 325°F. Lightly prick the bottom of each tartlet shell with fork tines. Place the baking sheet in the oven and bake the tartlet shells until light golden brown, about 15 minutes. Let cool completely on the baking sheet on a wire rack while you make the filling.

To make the filling, in a small saucepan over medium heat, combine the milk and water and bring to a boil, then remove from the heat. In a bowl, whisk together the eggs and egg yolk, sugar, salt, and lemon juice until the sugar dissolves and the mixture is well combined, about 1 minute. While whisking constantly, gradually pour the hot milk mixture into the egg mixture in a slow, steady stream, continuing to whisk until fully combined. Whisk in the vanilla. Pour the custard through a fine-mesh sieve into a large measuring pitcher.

Pour the custard into the baked tartlet shells, filling each to within ⅛ inch of the rim. Bake until the centers are just set, 15–20 minutes. Do not let the custard brown. The filling will puff up but will flatten when the tartlets cool. Let cool completely on the baking sheet on a wire rack, then carefully lift each tartlet from its pan. Serve at room temperature. The tartlets can be stored in an airtight container in the refrigerator for up to 3 days.

Pocahontas Spinning Arrow Salted Honey Pie

Grandmother Willow is a spiritual talking willow tree from whom Pocahontas seeks advice. After Pocahontas tells Grandmother Willow about her dream of a spinning arrow and her confusion about her path in life, she realizes that John's compass is the spinning arrow, which ultimately leads to her destiny. This silky pie, made with a crunchy, gluten-free crust and sweetened with honey and coconut sugar, is your destiny. Lemon and vanilla flavor the filling and a sprinkle of flaky salt on top offsets the sweetness.

Single-Crust Gluten-Free Pie Dough (page 129)

Tapioca flour for rolling the dough

For the Filling

¾ cup honey

½ cup coconut sugar

½ cup (1 stick) unsalted butter, melted and cooled

½ cup heavy cream

3 large eggs, lightly beaten

2 teaspoons fresh lemon juice

1 teaspoon pure vanilla extract

¼ teaspoon salt

2 tablespoons cornstarch

Flaky sea salt for sprinkling

Confectioners' sugar for dusting (optional)

Makes 8 servings

Make and refrigerate the pie dough as directed.

Have ready 2 large sheets of waxed paper. Dust the dough disk on both sides with tapioca flour, then place it between the waxed paper sheets on a work surface. Roll out the dough into a round 12 inches in diameter and about ⅛ inch thick. If the dough tears, press it back together. Peel away the top sheet of waxed paper and, using the bottom sheet, lift and invert the dough round into a 9-inch pie dish. Gently peel away the paper. Using your fingers, gently press the dough onto the bottom and up the sides of the dish. Using kitchen scissors or a small knife, trim the edge, leaving a 1-inch overhang. Fold the dough under itself to create an edge on the rim. To make a decorative edge, flute the dough with your index finger and thumb or crimp with fork tines. Refrigerate the piecrust for 30 minutes or freeze for 15 minutes.

Preheat the oven to 350°F. Lightly prick the bottom of the piecrust with fork tines. Line the crust with parchment paper and fill with pie weights. Bake the crust for 15 minutes, then remove from the oven and remove the weights and parchment. Return the crust to the oven and bake until it looks dry and is lightly golden, 10–13 minutes longer. Let cool on a wire rack. Leave the oven on.

While the crust is baking, make the filling. In a bowl, whisk together the honey, coconut sugar, butter, cream, eggs, lemon juice, vanilla, and salt. Sift the cornstarch over the top, then whisk until incorporated. Pour the filling into the crust.

Bake the pie until puffed and golden brown, 45–50 minutes, covering the edges with aluminum foil if they begin to brown too quickly. Let cool completely on a wire rack. Serve at room temperature or chilled. Sprinkle lightly with flaky sea salt and confectioners' sugar, if using, just before serving.

CHAPTER 3

Cakes & Cupcakes

Aladdin One-Jump Cakes

To keep from going hungry, Aladdin has to steal food and is constantly outsmarting and outrunning the law, always staying "One Jump Ahead." The addition of almond flour and pistachios makes these gluten-free cakes moist and tender, while rose water gives them a delicate floral flavor. To make them extra special, top each one with a sugared rose petal.

Nonstick cooking spray

½ cup almond flour

½ cup pistachios, toasted

⅓ cup granulated sugar

¼ cup white rice flour

1 teaspoon baking powder

¼ teaspoon salt

3 large egg whites

½ cup (1 stick) unsalted butter, melted and cooled

1 teaspoon rose water

Confectioners' sugar for dusting

Sugared rose petals for decorating (optional; see note)

Makes 24 mini cakes

Recipe Twist

No roses? Top these cakes with a fresh pitted cherry or a fresh raspberry.

Preheat the oven to 350°F. Spray a 24-cup mini muffin pan with cooking spray.

In a food processor, combine the almond flour, pistachios, granulated sugar, rice flour, baking powder, and salt and process until very finely ground, about 2 minutes. Transfer to a bowl.

Add the egg whites to the flour mixture and whisk until well combined. Add the butter in three additions, whisking well after each addition. Whisk in the rose water until blended.

Spoon the batter into the prepared muffin cups, dividing it evenly and filling the cups nearly full. Let sit for 10 minutes. Bake the cakes until lightly golden brown around the edges, about 15 minutes. Let cool in the pan on a wire rack for 5 minutes, then invert the pan onto the rack, lift off the pan, and let the cakes cool completely.

Arrange the cakes, bottom side up, on a large plate and, using a fine-mesh sieve, dust with confectioners' sugar. If you like, decorate each cake with a rose petal before serving.

Sugared Rose Petals

To make sugared rose petals, whisk an egg white just until evenly fluid but not foamy, then lightly "paint" edible (pesticide-free) rose petals with the egg white and sprinkle with superfine sugar. Set aside on a wire rack to dry. The sugared petals are best the day they are made.

Snow White Woodland Creature Spice Cake

Banished to the forest because of the Evil Queen's jealousy, Snow White finds solace in the home of the Seven Dwarfs and becomes friends with all the adorable forest creatures to whom she sings daily. This spiced cake, layered with honeyed frosting, stays beautifully moist with applesauce. Decorate it simply with rosemary sprigs, or go all out and top it with iced sugar cookies (page 131) baked in the shapes of Snow White's woodland friends. Either way, this cake will make you feel like dancing and singing in the forest.

¾ cup (1½ sticks) unsalted butter, plus more for the pan

2 cups cake flour, plus more for the pan

1½ teaspoons baking soda

1 teaspoon baking powder

¾ teaspoon ground cinnamon

¾ teaspoon ground cardamom

¼ teaspoon salt

1¼ cups firmly packed light brown sugar

3 large eggs

1 teaspoon pure vanilla extract

1 cup unsweetened applesauce, pear sauce, or a mixture, at room temperature

⅔ cup whole milk, at room temperature

Vanilla Sugar Cookies (page 131)

Cookie Icing (page 130)

Whipped Honey Frosting (page 130)

Rosemary sprigs for decorating (optional)

Makes 10–12 servings

Preheat the oven to 350°F. Butter two 8-inch round cake pans, then line the bottom of each pan with parchment paper and butter the parchment. Dust the pans with flour and tap out the excess.

In a medium bowl, mix together the flour, baking soda, baking powder, cinnamon, cardamom, and salt. In a large bowl, using an electric mixer, beat together the butter and sugar on medium-high speed until light and fluffy, about 3 minutes. Add the eggs one at a time, beating well after each addition. Add the vanilla and beat until blended. Turn off the mixer and scrape down the bowl with a rubber spatula.

In a liquid measuring pitcher, mix together the applesauce and milk. Add about one-third of the flour mixture to the butter mixture and beat on low speed just until combined. Pour in about half of the applesauce mixture and beat just until combined. Add about half of the remaining flour mixture and beat just until blended. Pour in the remaining applesauce mixture followed by the remaining flour mixture, beating after each addition just until combined. Turn off the mixer and scrape down the bowl, then give the batter a final stir with the spatula.

Divide the batter evenly between the prepared pans, spreading it in an even layer. Bake the cakes until golden and a toothpick inserted into the center comes out clean, 40–45 minutes. Leave the oven on for the cookies. Let cool in the pans on wire racks for 15 minutes, then invert the pans onto the racks, lift off the pans, and peel off the parchment from the cakes. Turn the cakes right side up and let cool completely.

Make the sugar cookies, cutting out the dough in the shape of forest animals. After they are baked and cooled completely, make the icing and decorate the cookies in different colors. Set the cookies aside until the icing sets, about 20 minutes. Meanwhile, make the Whipped Honey Frosting.

Continued on page 76

Using a long, serrated knife, cut each cooled cake layer in half horizontally to create 4 layers total. Place the bottom of 1 cake layer, cut side up, on a cake plate. Using an offset or icing spatula, spread some frosting over the top, making a thin, even layer about ¼ inch thick. Place the top of the same cake layer, cut side down, on top of the frosting, lining up the sides of the layers. Spread some frosting over the top the same way. Top with the bottom of the second layer, cut side cut, and spread some frosting over the top the same way. Place the top of the second layer, cut side down, on top and spread a thick layer of frosting over the top. Spread the remaining frosting around the sides of the cake, creating a sheer coating that allows the sides of the cake to peek through. Decorate the sides and top of the cake with the animal cookies and place the rosemary sprigs, if using, into the cake so they are sticking up like trees. Leftovers can be stored in an airtight container for up to 7 days.

Kakamora Coconut and Mango Cake

The curse of Te Fiti's missing heart causes the food systems on the islands to slowly disappear, which galvanizes Moana to embark on a quest to find the heart and undo the catastrophic damage to her island home. Sweet coconut, fresh mango, and tangy lime juice give this tropical loaf cake bold, fresh flavor that will transport you to a sun-drenched island cooled by ocean breezes. For a party, top each slice with a dollop of whipped cream (page 131).

For the Cake

Nonstick cooking spray

1½ cups all-purpose flour, plus more for the pan

1½ teaspoons baking powder

½ teaspoon salt

½ cup (1 stick) unsalted butter, at room temperature

¾ cup sugar

2 large eggs

1½ teaspoons pure coconut extract

½ teaspoon pure vanilla extract

½ cup whole milk

1 cup sweetened shredded dried coconut, lightly toasted

For the Topping

2 large ripe mangoes

2 teaspoons fresh lime juice

1–2 tablespoons sugar

1 tablespoon sweetened shredded dried coconut, lightly toasted

Makes 8 servings

To make the cake, position an oven rack in the lower third of the oven and preheat to 325°F. Coat a 9 x 5 x 3-inch loaf pan with cooking spray. Dust the pan with flour, then tap out the excess.

In a medium bowl, sift together the flour, baking powder, and salt. In a large bowl, using an electric mixer, beat together the butter and sugar on medium speed until pale and fluffy, about 3 minutes. Add the eggs one at a time, beating well after each addition. Add the coconut and vanilla extracts and beat until blended. Turn off the mixer and scrape down the bowl with a rubber spatula. Add half of the flour mixture and beat on low speed just until combined. Then add half of the milk and beat just until combined. Repeat with the remaining flour and milk. Turn off the mixer and stir in the shredded coconut with a spoon.

Scrape the batter into the prepared pan and smooth the top. Bake the cake until the top is golden and the center is firm to the touch, 55–60 minutes. Let cool in the pan on a wire rack for about 20 minutes, then turn out of the pan and let cool completely.

To make the topping, stand a mango on one of its narrow sides on a cutting board. Using a large, sharp knife, cut just slightly to one side of the center (you want to cut as close to the pit as possible), slicing downward to remove the flesh from the large, flat pit. Rotate the mango 180 degrees and cut the flesh away from the pit on the opposite side the same way. Using a small, sharp knife, peel the mango flesh, then cut into ¼-inch cubes. Transfer the cubes to a bowl. Repeat with the remaining mango and add to the bowl. Sprinkle the mango cubes with the lime juice and sugar to taste and toss to mix evenly.

To serve, slice the cake and accompany each slice with a spoonful of the mango mixture topped with a sprinkle of the coconut.

Ariel Mermaid Cupcakes

Inspired by the colorful, vivacious Ariel, a colorful cake batter whorled with pink, blue, and purple is swirled right in the pan, while the tinted frostings are combined in a pastry bag to create the gorgeous multicolor effect. Can't find mermaid sprinkles? Use star-shaped and glittery sprinkles to bring out your inner mermaid.

2 cups all-purpose flour

2 teaspoons baking powder

½ teaspoon baking soda

½ teaspoon salt

½ cup plus 2 tablespoons (1¼ sticks) unsalted butter, at room temperature

1 cup sugar

2 large eggs

2 teaspoons pure vanilla extract

1⅓ cups buttermilk

Red, blue and green gel food coloring

Fluffy Vanilla Frosting (page 130)

Mermaid sprinkles for decorating

Makes 18 cupcakes

Preheat the oven to 375°F. Line 18 standard muffins cups with paper liners.

In a medium bowl, mix together the flour, baking powder, baking soda, and salt. In a large bowl, using an electric mixer, beat together the butter and sugar on medium-high speed until light and fluffy, about 3 minutes. Add the eggs one at a time, beating well after each addition. Add the vanilla and beat until blended. Turn off the mixer and scrape down the bowl with a rubber spatula. Add about half of the flour mixture and beat on low speed just until combined. Then add the buttermilk and beat just until combined. Add the remaining flour mixture and beat just until combined. Turn off the mixer, scrape down the bowl, and then give the batter a final stir. The batter will be thick.

Scoop one-third of the batter into a small bowl, and another one-third of the batter into a second small bowl. Add 4 drops of red food coloring to the batter in 1 small bowl to color it pink, and 4 drops each of red coloring and blue food coloring to the batter in the other small bowl to color it purple. Using the rubber spatula, gently fold the food coloring into each bowl of batter.

Spoon the plain batter remaining in the large bowl into the prepared muffin cups, dividing it evenly. Spoon the pink batter into the cups, dividing it evenly, then spoon the purple batter into the cups, dividing it evenly. Swirl a wooden skewer or chopstick through the batter in each cup in a series of figure eights to create a marbled effect, being careful not to overmix the batters.

Bake the cupcakes until light golden brown and a toothpick inserted into the center of a cupcake comes out clean, about 17 minutes. Let cool in the pans on wire racks for 10 minutes, then carefully transfer the cupcakes to the rack and let cool completely.

To frost the cupcakes, divide the frosting evenly among 2 small bowls. Add 2 drops of blue food coloring to 1 bowl, then mix with a rubber spatula until the frosting is tinted pink. Add 2 drops of blue food coloring and 1 drop of green food coloring to the second bowl and mix until the frosting is tinted blue-green.

Fit a pastry bag with a small star tip. Spoon the blue-green frosting into the bag, keeping it on one side of filling only half of the bag. Then spoon the blue frosting into the bag, keeping it to another side and filling the other half of the bag. Twist the top of the bag closed and pipe a swirl of frosting onto each cupcake, then decorate each swirl with sprinkles. Serve right away, or cover and refrigerate for up to a day before serving.

Tiana New Orleans Doberge Cake

This tall, regal multilayered cake is fit for a queen—or a princess. A classic New Orleans dessert (and a cousin to the Hungarian Dobos torte), it consists of six layers of vanilla cake filled with creamy chocolate custard. The towering cake is then covered with a thin layer of chocolate buttercream followed by a shiny dark chocolate glaze.

For the Custard

⅓ cup granulated sugar

3 tablespoons unsweetened natural cocoa powder

2½ tablespoons cornstarch

Pinch of salt

¼ cup heavy cream

2¼ cups whole milk

5 oz semisweet or bittersweet chocolate, finely chopped

1 teaspoon pure vanilla extract

For the Cake

Nonstick cooking spray

3½ cups cake flour

1½ tablespoons baking powder

½ teaspoon baking soda

¾ teaspoon salt

1¼ cups (2½ sticks) unsalted butter, at room temperature

1⅔ cups granulated sugar

5 large eggs

2 large egg yolks

1 tablespoon pure vanilla extract

½ cup buttermilk

1 cup sour cream

(continued on page 82)

To make the custard, in a saucepan, sift together the granulated sugar, cocoa powder, cornstarch, and salt. Add the cream and ¼ cup of the milk and stir until smooth. Slowly add the remaining 2 cups milk, whisking constantly until smooth. Place the pan over medium heat and bring the mixture to a simmer, stirring constantly with the whisk. Continue to simmer, stirring constantly and reducing the heat slightly if the mixture begins to boil, until the custard is thick enough to coat the back of a spoon, about 6 minutes. Remove from the heat, add the chocolate, and stir until it melts and the mixture is smooth. Stir in the vanilla. Transfer to a bowl, cover with a piece of plastic wrap, pressing it directly onto the surface, and let cool to room temperature, then refrigerate until cold, at least 2 hours or up to 2 days.

To make the cake, preheat the oven to 350°F. Spray three 9-inch round cake pans with cooking spray. Line the bottom of each pan with parchment paper and lightly spray the parchment.

In a medium bowl, sift together the flour, baking powder, baking soda, and salt. In a large bowl, using an electric mixer, beat together the butter and granulated sugar on medium speed until light and fluffy, about 3 minutes. Add the whole eggs and yolks one at a time, beating well after each addition. Add the vanilla and beat until blended. Turn off the mixer and scrape down the bowl with a rubber spatula. On low speed, add one-third of the flour mixture, then the buttermilk, then half of the remaining flour mixture, then the sour cream, and finally the remaining flour mixture, beating after each addition just until combined. Turn off the mixer and scrape down the bowl, then beat again on low speed for 10 seconds.

Divide the batter evenly among the prepared pans, spreading it in an even layer (a thin offset spatula works well). Bake the cakes until lightly browned around the edges and a toothpick inserted into the center comes out clean, 24–28 minutes. Let cool in the pans on wire racks for 15 minutes, then invert the cakes onto the racks, lift off the pans, and peel off the parchment. Turn the cakes right side up and let cool completely.

Continued on page 82

Tiana New Orleans Doberge Cake *continued from page 81*

For the Frosting

½ cup (1 stick) unsalted butter,
at room temperature

1½ cups confectioners'
sugar, sifted

1 teaspoon pure vanilla extract

4 oz semisweet or bittersweet
chocolate, melted and cooled

2 teaspoons whole milk,
plus more if needed

For the Glaze

⅔ cup heavy cream

10 oz semisweet or bittersweet
chocolate, chopped

2 tablespoons light corn syrup

1 teaspoon pure vanilla extract

Makes about 8 servings

Using a long, serrated knife, cut each cake layer in half horizontally to create 6 layers total. Place a 9-inch cardboard circle or the removable bottom portion of a tart pan on a wire rack, then set 1 cake layer, bottom side down, on the circle or pan bottom. Spoon about ½ cup of the custard onto the cake layer and, using an icing or offset spatula, spread it to the edge. Place another cake layer, cut side up, on top and again spread with ½ cup of the custard. Repeat with the remaining 4 cake layers, layering them with the custard and ending with a cake layer bottom side up. Refrigerate while you make the frosting.

To make the frosting, in a bowl, using the electric mixer, beat the butter on medium speed until fluffy, 1–2 minutes. Add the confectioners' sugar and beat until light and fluffy, about 2 minutes. Add the vanilla and beat until blended. Reduce the speed to low, add the cooled chocolate, and beat until incorporated, then increase the speed to medium and beat until light and fluffy, about 2 minutes. Add the milk and beat until blended. The frosting should be easily spreadable; if it is too stiff, add more milk, ½ teaspoon at a time, as needed for a good consistency.

Using an offset or icing spatula, carefully spread the frosting in a thin, even layer over the top and down the sides of the cake. Refrigerate until the frosting is set, at least 30 minutes or up to overnight.

To make the glaze, in a saucepan over low heat, warm the cream. Add the chocolate and corn syrup and stir gently with a whisk until the chocolate is melted and the glaze is smooth. Let cool to room temperature, then stir in the vanilla.

Set a wire rack in a rimmed baking sheet, then place the cake on the rack. Using the offset or icing spatula, spread the glaze over the top and down the sides of the cake; work quickly before the glaze sets. Refrigerate the cake, uncovered, for at least 30 minutes or up to 2 days before serving. If the cake has been refrigerated for more than one hour, let it sit at room temperature for at least 1 hour before serving.

Belle Last Petal Cupcakes

It's a race against time to give and receive true love before the last petal on the enchanted rose falls and the Beast is cursed forevermore. These extra-citrusy gems, boasting lemon in both the cupcakes and the glaze, are each decorated with a strawberry rose that is sure to enchant your family and friends.

For the Cupcakes

1¼ cups all-purpose flour

½ teaspoon baking powder

½ teaspoon baking soda

¼ teaspoon salt

4 tablespoons (½ stick) unsalted butter, at room temperature

¾ cup granulated sugar

2 teaspoons grated lemon zest

1 large egg

¾ cup sour cream

For the Glaze

1 cup confectioners' sugar, sifted

2 tablespoons fresh lemon juice, plus more if needed

12 fresh strawberries for decorating

Makes 12 cupcakes

Recipe Twist

Serving these for a party? Arrange the mini cakes on a cake stand and sprinkle fresh mint leaves around the cakes on the stand.

Preheat the oven to 325°F. Line 12 standard muffin cups with paper liners.

To make the cupcakes, in a medium bowl, mix together the flour, baking powder, baking soda, and salt. In a large bowl, using an electric mixer, beat together the butter, granulated sugar, and lemon zest on medium speed until fluffy and pale, about 3 minutes. Add the egg and beat until combined. Turn off the mixer and scrape down the bowl with a rubber spatula. Add half of the flour mixture and beat on low speed just until combined. Then add the sour cream and beat just until combined. Add the remaining flour mixture and beat just until combined. Turn off the mixer, scrape down the bowl, and give the batter a final stir.

Spoon the batter into the prepared muffin cups, dividing it evenly and filling each cup about three-fourths full. Bake the cupcakes until golden brown and a toothpick inserted into the center of a cupcake comes out clean, 18–20 minutes. Let cool in the pan on a wire rack for 10 minutes, then carefully transfer the cupcakes to the rack and let cool completely.

To make the glaze, in a bowl, whisk together the confectioners' sugar and lemon juice until smooth and spreadable, adding more lemon juice as needed to achieve a good consistency. Spoon some icing on top of each cooled cupcake and, using the back of the spoon, spread it to the edge. Let the icing stand for 1–2 minutes until it sets.

To make strawberry roses, hull and core the strawberries. Working with one at a time, set the berry stem end down on a clean cutting board and, using a paring knife, make a shallow cut near the base of the berry. Using the edge of the knife, press down gently on the cut to fan the petal outward. Repeat, making as many petals around the base of the berry as desired. Cut and fan another row of petals slightly above the first row, layering them between the petals of the first row. Cut and fan a final row of petals near the tip of the berry. Make a shallow cut at the tip of the strawberry and, using the edge of the knife, gently nudge the top petals apart. Repeat with the remaining strawberries, then place a strawberry rose on top of each iced cupcake. These are best eaten the same day they are baked.

Mulan Avalanche Ice Cream Cake

During a battle against the Huns, Mulan cleverly uses a cannon to set off an avalanche on a distant snow-covered mountain, burying most of the enemy so she and her fellow warriors can escape. This sculptural cake recreates that snowy mountain with an avalanche of whipped cream and marshmallows. The cakes can be baked and layered up to 2 days before frosting and decorating.

For the Cake

Nonstick cooking spray

1 cup plus 2 tablespoons unsweetened natural cocoa powder

1½ cups boiling water

2½ cups all-purpose flour

2 teaspoons baking soda

½ teaspoon salt

14 tablespoons (1¾ sticks) unsalted butter, at room temperature

2 cups sugar

4 large eggs

2 teaspoons pure vanilla extract

2 cups buttermilk

3 quarts favorite ice cream, such as chocolate, chocolate chip, or cookie dough

For the Whipped Cream

3 cups heavy cream

¼ cup sugar

2 teaspoons pure vanilla extract

About 1 cup miniature marshmallows

Makes about 20 servings

A day before serving, make the cake. Preheat the oven to 350°F. Grease two 9-inch round cake pans and two 6-inch round cake pans with cooking spray, then line the bottom of each pan with parchment paper. Sift the cocoa into a heatproof bowl, then slowly add the boiling water, whisking until well mixed. Set aside to cool.

In a medium bowl, sift together the flour, baking soda, and salt. In a large bowl, using an electric mixer, beat together the butter and sugar on medium speed until pale and fluffy, about 3 minutes. Beat in the eggs one at a time, beating well after each addition. Add the cocoa mixture and vanilla and beat until blended. Turn off the mixer and scrape down the bowl with a rubber spatula. Add about one-third of the flour and beat on low speed just until combined. Then add half of the buttermilk and beat just until combined. Turn off the mixer and scrape down the bowl. Add half of the remaining flour, followed by the remaining buttermilk, and then all of the remaining flour, beating after the first two additions just until combined and then beating until smooth after the final addition, stopping the mixer to scrape down the bowl once or twice.

Divide the batter evenly among the prepared pans, filling all 4 pans to the same level. The 9-inch pans will require a little more batter than the 6-inch pans. Smooth the tops with the rubber spatula. Bake the cakes until they begin to pull away from the sides of the pans and a toothpick inserted into the center comes out clean, 33–36 minutes. Let cool in the pans on wire racks for 15 minutes, then invert the pans onto the racks, lift off the pans, and peel off the parchment. Turn the cakes right side up and let cool completely.

Let the ice cream sit at room temperature until it is just soft enough to spread, about 15 minutes. Meanwhile, using a serrated knife, slice a thin layer off the top of each cooled cake to create a flat surface. Line a clean 9-inch cake pan and a clean 6-inch cake pan with plastic wrap, allowing it to overhang the sides by several inches. Place one 9-inch cake layer, bottom side down, into the lined 9-inch cake pan, and one 6-inch cake layer, bottom side down, into the lined 6-inch cake pan. Top each cake layer with a thick layer of ice cream; about 2 quarts for the 9-inch cake and 1 quart for the 6-inch cake. The ice cream layer should come to just below or to the rim of the cake pan. Top with the second cake layer of each size, bottom side up, and press gently together.

Continued on page 89

Mulan Avalanche Ice Cream Cake continued from page 86

Wrap the overhanging plastic wrap up and around the cake layers, covering them completely. Freeze the cakes until firm, at least 4 hours or up to 2 days.

When ready to assemble, make the whipped cream. In a bowl, using the electric mixer, beat together the cream, sugar, and vanilla on medium-high speed to thick, stiff peaks. Do not overwhip.

Remove both cakes from the freezer. Using the plastic wrap, lift the 9-inch cake from the cake pan, then pull away and discard the plastic wrap. Place the cake on a cake plate or serving board and frost the top and sides with a layer of whipped cream.

Remove the 6-inch cake from the cake pan the same way and discard the plastic wrap. Carve a wide wedge into the cake at a slight angle, so the cake is wider at the top (4 inches) and smaller at the bottom (3 inches). Set the wedge aside. Place the 6-inch cake on top of the 9-inch cake, lining up one side of the 6-inch cake with the edge of the 9-inch cake so the 6-inch cake is offset. Frost the top and sides of the 6-inch cake with whipped cream. Place the wedge of removed cake on top of the 6-inch cake so it looks like a mountain peak, then frost it with whipped cream.

Spoon the remaining whipped cream into a piping bag fitted with a large round tip. Pipe "snowballs" around the bottom edge of both cakes and then pipe a broad, thick ribbon of cream down through the carved out wedge of the 6-inch cake and onto the 9-inch cake to resemble an avalanche. Add the marshmallows all along the carved out edge and across and down the 9-inch cake to the base and serving plate; they should look like falling snowballs.

Return the assembled cake to the freezer until ready to serve for up to overnight. Let stand at room temperature for about 15 minutes before cutting into wedges and serving.

Aurora Black Forest Cake

In the early nineteenth century, a version of the tale of Sleeping Beauty was made popular by Germany's Brothers Grimm. This Black Forest cake, a paean to that early work, is based on the classic German Kirschtorte (cherry torte), with layers of chocolate sponge cake, whipped cream, and cherries. Decorate this towering cake with chocolate brambles to recall the thicket of brambles that surrounds the castle after Aurora falls under Maleficent's sleeping curse.

For the Cake

Unsalted butter for the pan

1 cup all-purpose flour, plus more for the pan

⅔ cup Dutch-process cocoa powder

¼ teaspoon salt

9 large eggs, separated, at room temperature

1¾ cups sugar

1 teaspoon pure vanilla extract

½ teaspoon cream of tartar

For the Filling

1 lb fresh Bing cherries, pitted, or 1½ cups frozen pitted dark sweet cherries, thawed with liquid reserved

2 tablespoons granulated sugar

½ cup water or liquid from thawing frozen cherries

3 recipes Whipped Cream (page 131)

For the Chocolate Brambles

4 oz bittersweet chocolate chips

Makes about 16 servings

To make the cake, preheat the oven to 325°F. Butter two 9-inch round cake pans. Line the bottom of each pan with parchment paper and butter the parchment. Dust with flour and tap out the excess.

In a medium bowl, mix together the flour, cocoa powder, and salt. In a large bowl, using an electric mixer, beat together the egg yolks and 1 cup of the sugar on medium speed until light and fluffy, about 3 minutes. Add the vanilla and beat until blended. Turn off the mixer and wash and dry the beaters.

In another large bowl, beat together the egg whites and cream of tartar on medium speed until the whites are frothy. Slowly add the remaining ¾ cup sugar and continue to beat until stiff, glossy peaks form. Turn off the mixer. Using a rubber spatula, gently fold one-third of the egg whites into the egg yolk mixture until almost incorporated. Fold half of the flour mixture into the egg yolk mixture just until incorporated. Then fold in half of the remaining whites, followed by all of the remaining flour mixture. Finally, fold in the remaining whites just until the batter is smooth and no white streaks are visible.

Divide the batter evenly between the prepared pans. Bake the cakes until a toothpick inserted into the center comes out clean, about 35 minutes. Immediately run a small, thin-bladed knife around the inside edge of each pan to loosen the cake, pressing the knife against the pan, then let the cakes cool in the pans on wire racks for 10 minutes. Invert the cakes onto the racks, lift off the pans, and peel off the parchment. Turn the cakes right side up and let cool completely.

To make the filling, in a saucepan, combine the cherries, sugar, and water. If using the liquid from thawing frozen cherries, add water as needed to total ½ cup. Place the pan over medium heat and bring to a simmer, stirring until the sugar dissolves. Cover and simmer for 10 minutes. Remove from the heat and drain the cherries through a fine-mesh sieve placed over a heatproof bowl. Reserve the cherries and syrup separately.

To assemble the cake, using a long, serrated knife, cut each layer in half horizontally. You should have a total of 4 layers. Place 1 layer, cut side up, on a cake plate. Using a pastry brush, coat the top of the layer generously with some of the cherry syrup. Then, using a rubber spatula, spread one-fourth of the whipped cream evenly on the layer. Arrange one-third of the reserved cherries in an even layer over the whipped cream, pressing them into the cream to level the filling. Repeat with 2 more cake layers, placing them cut side up, brushing with cherry syrup, and topping them each with one-fourth of the cream and one-third of the cherries. Place the remaining layer on top, cut side down, and brush the top and sides of the cake with the remaining syrup. Spread the remaining whipped cream over the top and down the sides.

To make the chocolate brambles, draw several tree branch patterns of various sizes on a sheet of plain white paper and cover the paper with a piece of plastic wrap or parchment paper. Put the chocolate into a small microwave-safe bowl and microwave for 25 seconds, then stir and continue to microwave, stopping to stir every 15 seconds, just until melted and smooth.

Let cool slightly, then transfer the melted chocolate to a piping bag fitted with a medium round tip. Working quickly, pipe thick lines of the chocolate onto the parchment, tracing the branch patterns. Let the chocolate set for 5 minutes, then pipe a second layer of chocolate over the first layer. Chill the chocolate for 10 minutes in the refrigerator, then carefully peel the parchment away from the branches. Place the chocolate brambles on the sides and the top of the cake and serve right away. Leftovers can be stored in an airtight container in the refrigerator for up to 5 days.

Motunui Chocolate Lava Cakes

After her heart is stolen, the island goddess Te Fiti becomes a terrifying lava demon named Te Kā. Despite Te Kā's malice, Moana perseveres and calms Te Kā's fury by singing. Once calmed, Moana is able to return the heart and transform Te Kā back into benevolent Te Fiti. These dark, molten chocolate cakes are anything but terrifying and will soothe your soul after the first bite.

4 tablespoons (½ stick) unsalted butter, cut into small pieces, plus more for the ramekins

2 tablespoons unsweetened natural cocoa powder, sifted, plus more for the ramekins

8 oz bittersweet chocolate, finely chopped

1 teaspoon pure vanilla extract

Pinch of salt

4 large egg yolks

6 tablespoons sugar

3 large egg whites

Whipped Cream (page 131) for serving

Makes 6 mini cakes

Recipe Twist

To make a dairy-free, naturally sweetened whipped topping, chill ¾ cup coconut cream overnight in the refrigerator. In a bowl, using an electric mixer on medium-high speed, whip it along with 1 teaspoon maple syrup and ¼ tsp pure vanilla extract until fluffy, about 3 minutes.

Preheat the oven to 400°F. Lightly butter six ¾-cup (6-oz) ramekins, then dust with cocoa powder and tap out the excess. Set the ramekins on a small rimmed baking sheet.

Combine the chocolate and butter in a microwave-safe bowl and microwave, stirring every 20 seconds, until melted and smooth. Stir in the vanilla and salt and set aside to cool slightly.

In a bowl, using an electric mixer, beat together the egg yolks, 3 tablespoons of the sugar, and the cocoa powder on medium-high speed until thick, about 1 minute. Add the chocolate mixture to the yolk mixture and beat until blended. The mixture will be very thick.

In a clean bowl, using clean beaters, beat the egg whites on medium-high speed until very foamy and thick, about 3 minutes. Sprinkle in the remaining 3 tablespoons sugar, increase the speed to high, and beat until firm, glossy peaks form. Spoon one-third of the beaten whites onto the chocolate mixture and stir just until blended. Gently fold in the remaining whites just until no white streaks remain. Spoon the batter into the prepared ramekins, dividing it evenly.

Bake the cakes until they puff up and the tops are cracked, about 13 minutes. The inside of the cracks will look very wet. Remove from the oven, let sit for 1–2 minutes, then serve right away in the ramekins, topped with a dollop of whipped cream. Or run a small knife around the inside of each ramekin, invert each cake onto a plate, and lift off the ramekin. Top with a dollop of whipped cream.

Evil Queen Apple Cupcakes

Even the Evil Queen wouldn't banish these delicious apple-studded cupcakes, which are transformed into shiny red apples by dipping their swirl of cream cheese frosting into red sparkling sugar and adding a mint leaf. Alternatively, use Fluffy Vanilla Frosting (page 130) tinted with red gel food coloring.

8 tablespoons (1 stick) unsalted butter, at room temperature

1 lb crisp-tart baking apples, such as Gala or Honeycrisp, peeled, cored, and cut into ½-inch chunks

2 tablespoons plus ¾ cup granulated sugar

1 cup all-purpose flour

¾ teaspoon baking powder

½ teaspoon salt

¼ teaspoon baking soda

½ teaspoon ground cinnamon

¼ teaspoon ground allspice

Pinch of ground nutmeg

2 large eggs

1 teaspoon pure vanilla extract

¼ cup sour cream

Cream Cheese Frosting (page 130)

About ½ cup red sparkling sugar for decorating

12 small fresh mint leaves for decorating

12 fresh mint stems, each ½ inch long, for decorating

Makes 12 cupcakes

Preheat the oven to 350°F. Line 12 standard muffin cups with paper liners.

In a saucepan over medium-high heat, melt 2 tablespoons of the butter. Add the apple chunks and 2 tablespoons of the granulated sugar and cook, stirring often, until the apples are tender and soft, about 5 minutes. Transfer the mixture to a bowl and let cool completely.

In a medium bowl, mix together the flour, baking powder, salt, baking soda, cinnamon, allspice, and nutmeg. In a large bowl, using an electric mixer, beat together the remaining 6 tablespoons butter and ¾ cup granulated sugar on medium-high speed until light and fluffy, about 3 minutes. Add the eggs one at a time, beating well after each addition. Add the vanilla and beat until blended. Turn off the mixer and scrape down the bowl with a rubber spatula. Add about half of the flour mixture and beat on low speed just until combined. Then add the sour cream and beat just until combined. Add the remaining flour mixture and beat just until combined. Turn off the mixer, add the apples, and mix with the spatula until evenly distributed.

Spoon the batter into the prepared muffin cups, dividing it evenly. Bake the cupcakes until golden brown and a toothpick inserted into the center of a cupcake comes out clean, 18–20 minutes. Let cool in the pans on wire racks for 5 minutes, then carefully transfer the cupcakes to the racks and let cool completely. (The cupcakes can be refrigerated in an airtight container for up to 3 days before decorating.)

Make the frosting. To decorate the cupcakes, using a small offset or icing spatula, spread a thick, smooth layer of the frosting on each cupcake, rounding the top. Pour the sparkling sugar into a small bowl. One at a time, turn each cupcake upside down and roll the frosting in the sugar, coating it completely red. Place a mint leaf and stem in the center of the frosting to simulate the stem and leaf of an apple. Serve at once.

Belle Teacup Cakes

The enchanted teacup, Chip Potts, is an endearing character in *Beauty and the Beast*. He ultimately helps save Belle and her father so they can free the Beast from Gaston and the unruly mob. Baked in oven-safe teacups, these delightful salted caramel cakes are an ode to sweet Chip. A drizzle of salted caramel and a dollop of whipped cream make them the ideal addition to any tea party.

For the Cakes

Nonstick cooking spray

1¼ cups all-purpose flour

¾ teaspoon baking powder

¼ teaspoon salt

½ cup (1 stick) unsalted butter, at room temperature

1 cup firmly packed dark brown sugar

2 large eggs

1 teaspoon pure vanilla extract

⅓ cup whole milk

For the Topping

⅓ cup store-bought caramel sauce

Pinch of salt

½ recipe Whipped Cream (page 131)

Makes 6 cakes

To make the cakes, preheat the oven to 350°F. Spray six ¾-cup (6-oz) oven-safe teacups or ramekins with cooking spray. Place on a small rimmed baking sheet.

In a medium bowl, mix together the flour, baking powder, and salt. In a large bowl, using an electric mixer, beat together the butter and sugar on medium speed until pale and fluffy, about 3 minutes. Beat in the eggs and vanilla until blended. Turn off the mixer and scrape down the bowl with a rubber spatula. Add half of the flour mixture and beat on low speed just until combined. Then add half of the milk and beat just until combined. Repeat with the remaining flour mixture and milk. Turn off the mixer, scrape down the bowl, and give the batter a final stir.

Spoon the batter into the prepared cups, dividing it evenly and filling each cup about two-thirds full. Bake the cakes until golden brown and a toothpick inserted into the center of a cake comes out clean, 30–35 minutes. Let cool completely, then remove the cakes from the cups.

To make the topping, put the caramel into a small microwave-safe bowl and microwave until warmed and pourable, about 20 seconds. Stir in the salt.

Spread the top of each cooled cake with about 1 tablespoon of the caramel sauce, top with a dollop of whipped cream, and serve.

Tiana King Cake

In *The Princess and the Frog*, Tiana and Naveen return from their adventures in the bayou to the midst of the Mardi Gras parade in New Orleans, seeking a way to transform Naveen back into human form. King cake, a staple of Mardi Gras, is a rich, sweet yeasted bread baked in the shape of a large ring and decorated with wide stripes of purple, green, and gold sparkling sugar, the traditional colors of Mardi Gras. An ovenproof charm, traditionally in the shape of a baby, is hidden inside each cake.

⅓ cup sugar

Grated zest of 1 lemon

4 cups all-purpose flour

1 package (2½ teaspoons) instant yeast

1 teaspoon salt

¾ cup (1½ sticks) cold unsalted butter, cut into cubes

3 large eggs

1 cup whole milk, warmed (110°F)

1 ovenproof charm, such as a Mardi Gras baby, or a whole almond

1 large egg yolk whisked with 1 tablespoon water for brushing

Purple, green, and gold or yellow decorating sugars

Makes 16 servings

Recipe Twist

A classic Mardi Gras dinner of jambalaya or gumbo ends with a slice of this colorfully striped cake. But the cake also makes a great after-school snack with a glass of milk.

In a food processor, combine the sugar and lemon zest and process for 15 seconds to mix well. Add the flour, yeast, and salt and process again for 15 seconds to mix well. Scatter the butter pieces evenly over the flour mixture, then push them down into the flour mixture. Pulse about 15 times, until the mixture resembles bread crumbs.

In a large liquid measuring pitcher or a bowl with a spout, whisk together the eggs and milk. With the processor running, pour the egg mixture through the feed tube and process for about 30 seconds, stopping to scrape down the sides of the processor if necessary. The dough should be soft and sticky.

Scrape the dough into a large bowl, cover tightly, and refrigerate overnight. It will stiffen as it chills to the consistency of a dense cookie dough.

Line a rimmed baking sheet with parchment paper. Working quickly, before the dough warms up and begins to soften, transfer the cold dough to the parchment and, using your hands, mold it into an oblong ring about 12 inches long and 2 inches wide with a hole in the center. Dampen your hands and pat the ring gently to smooth the surface. Push the charm into the underside of the dough to conceal it. Cover the dough ring loosely with another sheet of parchment. Set the pan in a warm, draft-free place and let rise until doubled in size, about 3 hours.

Preheat the oven to 375°F. Brush the surface of the dough gently and evenly with the egg yolk mixture. Sprinkle generously with the decorating sugars, alternating wide stripes of purple, green, and gold.

Bake the cake until golden brown, 25–30 minutes. Let cool on the pan on a wire rack for at least 10 minutes.

Transfer the cake to a cake plate. Serve warm or at room temperature, cut on the diagonal into thin slices.

Heihei Pineapple-Cherry Boat Snack Cakes

The strong and fearless teenage daughter of a Polynesian island chief, Moana sets out in a canoe to save her land and its people from a steadily growing darkness by returning a life-creating stone to the goddess Te Fiti. The yellow-red of these tropical cakes, inspired by Heihei, Moana's bumbling companion, is just the thing for an island-themed party. Use whatever type of jarred cherries you like, whether Morello or maraschino.

½ cup (1 stick) unsalted butter, melted, plus room-temperature butter for the muffin cups

¾ cup firmly packed light brown sugar

2 cans (8 oz) pineapple rings in juice (8 rings total), drained

8 jarred Morello cherries or other jarred cherries

For the Batter

1¼ cups cake flour

½ teaspoon baking soda

½ teaspoon salt

½ cup (1 stick) unsalted butter, at room temperature

¼ cup firmly packed light brown sugar

3 large eggs, separated, at room temperature

1 teaspoon pure vanilla extract

¾ cup buttermilk, at room temperature

¼ cup granulated sugar

Makes 8 mini cakes

Butter 8 jumbo muffin cups (each 1-cup capacity); you will need 2 muffin pans. Spoon 1 tablespoon melted butter into each prepared cup, then add 1½ tablespoons firmly packed brown sugar to each cup, spreading it evenly on the bottom. Lay 1 pineapple ring in each cup (you may need to cut the ring and overlap it slightly to make it fit), and place a cherry in the center of the ring. Preheat the oven to 325°F.

To make the batter, in a medium bowl, sift together the flour, baking soda, and salt. In a large bowl, using an electric mixer, beat together the butter and brown sugar on medium speed until pale and fluffy, about 2 minutes. Beat in the egg yolks and vanilla until well blended. Turn off the mixer and scrape down the bowl with a rubber spatula. Add about half of the flour mixture and beat on low speed just until combined. Add the buttermilk and beat until combined, then add the remaining flour mixture and beat just until well combined. Scrape down the bowl with the spatula. The batter will be thick.

In a clean bowl, using clean beaters, beat the egg whites on medium speed until soft peaks form, about 3 minutes. Slowly pour in the granulated sugar while continuing to beat until the mixture firms up slightly. The whites are ready if they fall over gently when the beaters are lifted. Using a rubber spatula, fold the egg whites into the batter just until no white streaks remain. Divide the batter evenly among the prepared muffin cups, filling each about three-fourths full.

Bake the cakes until they are golden brown and a toothpick inserted into the center of a cake comes out clean, about 25 minutes. The top should feel slightly firm to the touch. Let cool in the pans on wire racks for about 5 minutes. Invert a platter on top of a pan and, holding the plate and pan together, invert them. Gently pull off the pan, being careful not to burn yourself. Repeat with the second pan. Leftover cakes may be stored in an airtight container at room temperature for up to 5 days. Warm gently in the oven before serving.

Flit Hummingbird Cupcakes

Stubborn and devoted Flit the hummingbird is a friend of Pocahontas and sidekick to rascally Meeko the raccoon. These yummy cupcakes combine pineapple-and-banana-flavored hummingbird cake, a Jamaican original and Southern favorite, and rich, fluffy cream cheese frosting. If you have time, decorate them with hummingbird-shaped sugar cookies, making them perfect for a party. Just be careful Meeko doesn't try to steal them!

For the Cupcakes

1 cup all-purpose flour

½ cup sugar

1 teaspoon baking soda

½ teaspoon ground cinnamon

¼ teaspoon salt

1 large, ripe banana, peeled

½ cup canned crushed pineapple in juice, with juice

⅓ cup canola oil

1 large egg

1 teaspoon pure vanilla extract

⅓ cup chopped toasted pecans (optional)

For Decorating

½ recipe Vanilla Sugar Cookies (page 131; optional)

½ recipe Cookie Icing (page 130; optional)

½ recipe Cream Cheese Frosting (page 130)

Pink and green sprinkles (if not making cookies)

Makes 12 cupcakes

To make the cupcakes, preheat the oven to 350°F. Line 12 standard muffin cups with paper liners.

In a large bowl, mix together the flour, sugar, baking soda, cinnamon, and salt. In a medium bowl, using a fork, mash the banana to a purée; you should have about ¾ cup. Add the pineapple, oil, egg, and vanilla to the banana and mix well. Add the banana mixture to the flour mixture and stir just until combined. Stir in the pecans, if using.

Spoon the batter into the prepared muffin cups, dividing it evenly and filling each cup about three-fourths full. Bake the cupcakes until puffed and golden brown and a toothpick inserted into the center of a cupcake comes out clean, about 20 minutes. Let cool in the pan on a wire rack for 10 minutes, then carefully transfer the cupcakes to the rack and let cool completely.

If you like, make the sugar cookies, using a hummingbird cookie cutter (or a small knife and a handmade hummingbird pattern) to cut out the cookies from the dough. You will need 12 cookies, one for each cupcake. Make the cookie icing, color half of it green and a fourth of it pink, leaving the remaining fourth white. Apply the frosting to the cookies, coloring the back, wings and tail feathers of the bird green, the underside of the beak pink, and coloring the body white. Set the cookies aside until the icing sets, about 20 minutes.

Make the cream cheese frosting as directed. Using a small offset or icing spatula, or a pastry bag fitted with a large round tip, frost the cupcakes. If you made the cookies, top each cupcake with a hummingbird cookie. Alternatively, sprinkle the frosted cupcakes with green and pink sprinkles. Serve right away or store in an airtight container for up to 7 days.

Recipe Twist

Not in the mood for sprinkles? Decorate the cupcakes with your favorite chopped, toasted nut.

Merida Witch's Spell Cakes

When Merida and her mother have a falling out over a suitor for Merida, she runs away and meets a witch who gives her a spell to change her fate. The magical spell comes as a cake that Merida offers to her mother, transforming her (and ultimately her three little brothers) into a bear. The only spell these gluten-free, raspberry jam–topped almond cakes cast is to make the eater want another one.

Nonstick cooking spray

1¼ cups almond flour

½ cup cornstarch

2 teaspoons baking powder

7 oz almond paste

⅔ cup granulated sugar

Grated zest of 1 lemon

½ teaspoon salt

¾ cup (1½ sticks) unsalted butter, melted and cooled

4 large eggs, at room temperature

⅓ cup raspberry jam

Confectioners' sugar for dusting

Makes 16 mini cakes

Preheat the oven to 350°F. Spray 16 standard muffin cups with cooking spray.

In a bowl, mix together the almond flour, cornstarch, and baking powder. Using the small holes on a box grater-shredder, grate the almond paste into a large bowl. Add the sugar, lemon zest, and salt to the almond paste and, using an electric mixer, beat on medium-low speed until the almond paste breaks up and looks like bread crumbs, about 2 minutes. Increase the speed to medium-high, add the butter, and beat until smooth, about 2 minutes. Add the eggs one at a time, beating well and then stopping the mixer and scraping down the bowl after each addition. Beat on high speed until the mixture is fully blended, about 1 minute. Reduce the speed to low, add the almond flour mixture, and beat just until combined.

Spoon the batter into the prepared muffin cups, dividing it evenly and filling each cup about three-fourths full. Bake the cakes until golden brown and a toothpick inserted into the center of a cake comes out clean, about 18 minutes. Let cool in the pans on wire racks for about 10 minutes, then invert the cakes onto the racks and turn them right side up. Spoon about 1 teaspoon of the jam onto the center of each cake, smoothing it into a round. Let the cakes cool completely.

Just before serving, using a small fine-mesh sieve, dust the edge of each cake with confectioners' sugar. Leftover cakes will keep in an airtight container at room temperature for up to 7 days.

Pocahontas Colors of the Wind Cake

Inspired by Native American poetry, music, and folklore, "Colors of the Wind" was Pocahontas's tribute song to the earth and to the spiritual essence within everything in nature. As she sings that the wonders of the world are not something to be conquered, but rather something to respect and to live in harmony with, she is enveloped in the vibrant colors of nature. This pumpkin spice cake, with its center layer of toasted pecan streusel, is especially beautiful when decorated with a rainbow of leaf-shaped cookies that echo the colors of the wind. For a simpler version, decorate the cake with toasted pecan halves.

Nonstick cooking spray

For the Streusel

1 cup pecans, lightly toasted and chopped

½ cup all-purpose flour

⅓ cup firmly packed light brown sugar

1 teaspoon ground cinnamon

Pinch of salt

5 tablespoons unsalted butter, melted

For the Cake

1½ cups all-purpose flour

2 teaspoons baking powder

½ teaspoon baking soda

2 teaspoons ground cinnamon

1 teaspoon ground ginger

½ teaspoon salt

¼ teaspoon ground nutmeg

½ cup (1 stick) unsalted butter

⅔ cup firmly packed light brown sugar

2 large eggs

½ cup pumpkin purée

½ cup sour cream

For Decorating

½ recipe Vanilla Sugar Cookies (page 131; optional)

½ recipe Cookie Icing (page 130; optional)

½ recipe Cream Cheese Frosting (page 130)

16 pecan halves, toasted (optional; if not making cookies)

Preheat the oven to 350°F. Spray a 9 x 3-inch springform pan with cooking spray.

To make the streusel, in a bowl, mix together the pecans, flour, sugar, cinnamon, and salt. Using a fork, stir in the butter until the mixture is evenly moistened and begins to clump.

To make the cake, in a medium bowl, sift together the flour, baking powder, baking soda, cinnamon, ginger, salt, and nutmeg. In a large bowl, using an electric mixer, beat together the butter and sugar on medium-high speed until light and fluffy, about 3 minutes. Beat in the eggs one at a time, beating well after each addition. Turn off the mixer and scrape down the bowl with a rubber spatula. Add the pumpkin purée and sour cream and mix with the spatula until well blended. Add the flour mixture and stir until fully incorporated. The batter will be quite thick.

Add half of the batter to the prepared pan, spreading it evenly with the spatula. Sprinkle the streusel over the batter in an even layer. Dollop the remaining batter over the streusel and spread it in as even a layer as you can.

Bake the cake until a toothpick inserted into the center comes out clean, about 50 minutes. Let cool in the pan on a wire rack for 20 minutes. Unclasp and lift off the pan sides, then, using a wide metal spatula, slide the cake from the pan bottom onto the rack. Let cool completely.

If you like, make the sugar cookies, cutting out the dough in the shape of leaves. Make the icing and decorate the cookies in a rainbow of colors (the colors of the wind). Set the cookies aside until the icing sets, about 20 minutes.

Make the frosting. Using an offset or icing spatula, frost the top of the cake with a thick layer of the frosting. If you made the cookies, arrange them on the cake in a decorative pattern. Alternatively, decorate the top with the pecan halves. Serve right away. Leftovers can be stored in an airtight container in the refrigerator for up to 7 days.

Makes about 8 servings

Cinderella Pumpkin Carriage Cheesecake

An elegant carriage alone wasn't enough to get Cinderella to the ball, so with a flick of her wand, her Fairy Godmother changes Cinderella's mice friends into horses, Bruno the dog into a footman, and Major the horse into a coachman. With its crisp gingersnap crust and creamy spiced pumpkin filling, this cheesecake would be welcome at any royal ball.

For the Crust

2 cups gingersnap cookie crumbs

¼ cup firmly packed brown sugar

5 tablespoons unsalted butter, melted and cooled

For the Filling

2 lb cream cheese, at room temperature

1⅓ cups firmly packed light brown sugar

1 can (15 oz) pumpkin puree (about 1½ cups)

1 tablespoon pure vanilla extract

1½ teaspoons ground cinnamon

¼ teaspoon ground allspice

5 large eggs

Makes 12 servings

Preheat the oven to 350°F.

To make the crust, in a food processor, combine the gingersnap crumbs and brown sugar and process for several seconds to mix. Add the butter and process until the crumb-sugar mixture is evenly moistened and begins to stick together. Turn the crumb mixture out into a 9 by 3-inch springform pan. Drape your hand with plastic wrap to form a glove, then press the crumbs firmly onto the bottom and 2 inches up the sides of the pan.

Wrap aluminum foil around the outside of the pan. Bake the crust until set, about 10 minutes. Let cool completely on a wire rack.

To make the filling, in a large bowl, using an electric mixer, beat together the cream cheese and sugar on medium speed until well blended, about 3 minutes. Turn off the mixer and scrape down the bowl with a rubber spatula. Add the pumpkin purée, vanilla, cinnamon, and allspice and beat on medium speed until blended. Add the eggs one at a time, beating well after each addition. Turn off the mixer, scrape down the bowl, and give the batter a final stir with the spatula.

Pour the filling into the cooled crust, spreading it to the edges of the pan with the spatula. Bake the cheesecake until it puffs and the center is almost set, about 1½ hours. Cover and refrigerate until chilled, at least 3 hours.

Run a table knife around the inside edge of the pan to loosen the cake sides. Remove the foil from the pan and unclasp and lift off the pan sides. Then, using a wide metal spatula, slide the cake from the pan bottom onto a cake plate and serve. Leftovers can be stored in an airtight container in the refrigerator for up to 5 days.

Ariel's Secret Grotto Cake

Gadgets and gizmos, whosits and whatsits are what Ariel calls the treasures she hides away in her Secret Grotto. This rich chocolate Bundt cake is a treasure trove of delicious decadence topped with a sea-salt caramel drizzle. A slice of this cake is great with a scoop of vanilla ice cream or whipped cream (page 131).

4 tablespoons (½ stick) unsalted butter, plus more for the pan

1 cup all-purpose flour, plus more for the pan

3 oz bittersweet chocolate, coarsely chopped

1 cup granulated sugar

½ cup unsweetened natural cocoa powder

1½ teaspoons baking soda

¼ teaspoon salt

2 large eggs

1 cup buttermilk

2 teaspoons pure vanilla extract

2¼ cups store-bought caramel sauce

Flaky sea salt

Blue sparkling sugar (optional)

Makes 10–12 servings

Recipe Twist

Swap out the caramel sauce for a sugar-free raspberry compote: In a saucepan over medium heat, bring 4 cups fresh raspberries, ¼ cup pure maple syrup, 2 tbsp fresh lemon juice, and ½ cup water to a boil, then reduce to a simmer and cook, stirring occasionally, until the compote thickens, about 10 minutes.

Preheat the oven to 350°F. Butter a 10-cup Bundt pan, making sure to coat all the crevices. Dust with flour and tap out the excess.

In a saucepan over low heat, combine the butter and chocolate and melt slowly, stirring to combine. Remove from the heat and set aside.

In a large bowl, mix together the flour, sugar, cocoa powder, baking soda, and salt. Using an electric mixer on low speed, beat in the following ingredients one at a time, mixing just until combined after each addition: the chocolate mixture, eggs, buttermilk, and vanilla. Increase the speed to high and continue to beat until light and fluffy, about 3 minutes.

Pour the batter into the prepared pan. Bake the cake until a toothpick inserted near the center comes out clean, 40–45 minutes. Let cool in the pan on a wire rack for about 15 minutes, then invert the cake onto the rack, lift off the pan, and let the cake cool completely. (The cake can be baked and cooled up to 8 hours in advance. Loosely cover the cake and keep at room temperature.)

Set the cake on the rack in a rimmed baking sheet to catch any drips. Pour the caramel sauce over the top of the cake, allowing it to flow down the sides. Sprinkle lightly with sea salt and dust with sparkling sugar, if using. Carefully transfer the cake to a cake plate and serve.

Disney Castle Cake

What princess wouldn't want an iconic castle for her birthday? This epic two-tiered cake consists of layers of strawberry cake and vanilla cake sandwiched with creamy vanilla buttercream and jam. It's a labor of love, but the cakes can be baked up to 3 days in advance, then layered in tiers and coated with a thin layer of frosting before decorating. Fondant is available in a wide variety of colors, so pick your favorite (or buy white and tint it yourself). It's easy to work with and gives the cake a professional finish, plus it's great to use for embellishing your castle with as many decorative flourishes as you like.

For the Strawberry Cake

¾ lb fresh strawberries, hulled and roughly chopped

Nonstick cooking spray

2½ cups cake flour

1 tablespoon baking powder

¼ teaspoon baking soda

½ teaspoon salt

1 cup (2 sticks) unsalted butter, at room temperature

1½ cups granulated sugar

3 large eggs

1 teaspoon pure vanilla extract

A few drops pink gel food coloring (optional)

½ cup sour cream

½ cup whole milk

For the Vanilla Cake

2½ cups cake flour

1 tablespoon baking powder

¼ teaspoon baking soda

½ teaspoon salt

1 cup (2 sticks) unsalted butter, at room temperature

1½ cups granulated sugar

3 large eggs

2 teaspoons pure vanilla extract

1 cup sour cream

½ cup whole milk

To make the strawberry cake, put the strawberries into a blender and purée until smooth. Transfer to a small saucepan, place over medium-low heat, and cook, stirring often, until the purée thickens and is reduced to ½ cup, about 20 minutes. Remove from the heat and let cool completely. Transfer to an airtight container and refrigerate for at least 1 hour or up to 2 days.

Preheat the oven to 350°F. Spray a 10-inch square cake pan and a 6-inch square cake pan with cooking spray. Line the bottom of each pan with parchment paper and lightly spray the parchment.

In a medium bowl, sift together the flour, baking powder, baking soda, and salt. In a large bowl, using an electric mixer, beat together the butter and sugar on medium speed until light and fluffy, 3 minutes. Add the eggs one at a time, beating well after each addition. Add the vanilla and food coloring (if using) and beat until blended. Turn off the mixer and scrape down the bowl with a rubber spatula. Add about one-third of the flour mixture and beat on low speed just until combined. Add the sour cream and milk and beat just until combined. Add half of the remaining flour mixture, then the strawberry purée, and finally all of the remaining flour mixture, beating after each addition just until combined. Turn off the mixer and scrape down the bowl. Then beat again on low speed for 10 seconds.

Scrape about two-thirds of the batter into the prepared 10-inch pan and the remainder into the prepared 6-inch pan. Spread the batter in an even layer (a thin offset spatula works well); each layer should be about ½ inch thick. Bake the cakes until their edges pull away slightly from the sides of the pans and a toothpick inserted into the center of each cake comes out with crumbs, not batter, attached, 25–30 minutes. Let cool in the pans on wire racks for about 15 minutes, then invert the cakes onto the racks, lift off the pans, and peel off the parchment. Turn the cakes upright and let cool completely.

Continued on page 108

3 recipes Fluffy Vanilla Frosting
(page 130)

1 jar (13 oz) strawberry jam
(about 1 ¼ cups)

Confectioners' sugar for dusting

2 ½ lb store-bought white
vanilla fondant

For the Decorations

5 large sugar cones

About 1½ teaspoons whole milk
for thinning the frosting

About ½ cup rainbow nonpareils

5 strips construction paper
in 5 different colors, each
1 by 5 inches

Paper glue

5 wooden skewers

Gel food coloring in assorted
colors, such as purple, green,
blue, and brown

About 1 cup gumdrops or
miniature marshmallows

Serves 20 or more

Repeat to make the vanilla cake batter the same way, omitting the strawberry purée and adding the 1 cup sour cream after the first addition of the flour mixture and the ½ cup milk after the second addition of the flour mixture, then bake and cool as directed.

Make the frosting; transfer ¾ cup of the frosting to an airtight container and refrigerate for decorating.

Place the 10-inch strawberry cake layer, bottom side down, on a large, flat serving platter or tray. Using an offset or icing spatula, spread the top with a ¼-inch-thick layer of the frosting. Spread about three-fourths of the strawberry jam on top of the frosting in a thin, even layer. Top with the 10-inch vanilla cake layer, bottom side down. Spread a thin, smooth layer of the frosting over the top and down the sides of the cake. Refrigerate for at least 1 hour or up to overnight.

Place the 6-inch strawberry cake layer, bottom side down, on a flat plate or tray. Using an offset or icing spatula, spread the top with a ¼-inch-thick layer of the frosting. Spread the remaining strawberry jam on top in a thin, even layer. Top with the 6-inch vanilla cake layer, bottom side down. Spread a thin, smooth layer of the frosting over the top and down the sides of the cake. Refrigerate for at least 1 hour or up to overnight.

Dust a work surface with confectioners' sugar. Roll out 1½ lb of the fondant into a 16- or 17-inch square about ⅛ inch thick. Gently roll the fondant around the rolling pin, then unroll it over the 10-inch cake, covering the cake completely. Using a fondant smoother, smooth the fondant over the cake, starting in the center of the top and moving down the sides to the bottom. Trim away any excess fondant around the bottom edges. Shape and press the fondant around the square edges, smoothing them, then trim away any overhang. Reserve the scraps. Roll out ¾ lb of the fondant into a 12- or 13-inch square, then use to cover the 6-inch cake the same way, reserving the scraps. Transfer the 6-inch cake to the top of the 10-inch cake, centering it. Refrigerate the stacked cakes while you make the decorations.

To make the turrets, carefully cut the tip off of each sugar cone to create an opening just large enough to push a wooden skewer through. Remove the reserved ¾ cup frosting from the refrigerator and stir in the milk, a little at a time, just until the frosting is thin enough to spread easily. Put the nonpareils on a flat plate. Holding a cone from the inside with your fingers, and using a small offset or icing spatula, spread a very thin layer of the frosting all over the outside of the cone. Roll the cone in the nonpareils to coat completely, then set the cone aside on a large plate to dry. Repeat with the remaining sugar cones, adding them to the plate. Set the leftover frosting aside.

Fold a strip of the paper in half crosswise and cut out a triangle from the open end, creating a flag. Spread a thin layer of glue on the inside of each strip of paper, then wrap it around the skewer, pressing the paper together and the skewer tightly against the folded end. Repeat with the remaining paper strips and skewers.

Use the fondant scraps and the remaining ¼ lb fondant, which you can color with gel food coloring, to create decorations for the castle, such as a door, windows, and a narrow rope for edging the base of the top tier and the base of the turrets. To cut out shapes, dust the work surface with confectioners' sugar, roll out the fondant about ⅛ inch thick, and cut into desired shapes with a small, sharp knife. For the rope to use for edging, shape the fondant with your palms, rolling it back and forth on the sugar-dusted surface. To adhere the fondant decorations to the cake, lightly brush the back of each piece with water and then press firmly but gently into place.

To add the turrets, spread the wide edge of each cone with a little of the thinned frosting and place a cone on each corner of the larger cake and the fifth cone on the center of the smaller cake. Wrap a fondant rope around the base of each cone to hide the edge. Push a flag-topped wooden skewer through the hole in the top of each turret, pressing the skewer into the cake to secure firmly.

To add crenellations, spread one side of each gumdrop or marshmallow with some of the thinned frosting and arrange the gumdrops or marshmallows along the top edge of each cake.

Serve at once, cut into slices, or cover and refrigerate for up to 3 days.

Flora, Fauna, and Merryweather Fairy Cakes

The good fairies—Flora, Fauna, and Merryweather—watch over Aurora, softening Maleficent's curse and raising her in the forest until her sixteenth birthday. These pretty rose-scented cakes, their flavoring a nod to Briar Rose, the name the fairies give to Aurora when she is in hiding, are decorated with pink-hued icing and toasted pistachios. Edible dried or sugared rose petals (page 72) would also be an elegant touch.

For the Cakes

¾ cup (1½ sticks) unsalted butter, at room temperature

¾ cup granulated sugar

¼ teaspoon salt

1 tablespoon rose water

1½ teaspoons pure vanilla extract

3 large eggs

1½ cups self-rising flour

For the Icing

½ cup (1 stick) unsalted butter, at cool room temperature

3 cups confectioners' sugar, sifted

Pinch of salt

1 tablespoon rose water

1 teaspoon pure vanilla extract

3 drops pink, green, and/or blue food coloring

2 tablespoons finely chopped pistachios for sprinkling (optional)

Makes 12 small cakes

To make the cakes, preheat the oven to 350°F. Line 12 standard muffin cups with paper liners.

In a large bowl, using an electric mixer, beat together the butter, granulated sugar, and salt on medium speed until light and fluffy, about 3 minutes. Add the rose water and vanilla and beat until blended. Add the eggs one at a time, beating well after each addition. On low speed, gradually add the flour, beating just until incorporated.

Spoon the batter into the prepared muffin cups, dividing it evenly. Bake the cakes until golden and a toothpick inserted into the center of a cake comes out clean, 15–20 minutes. Let cool completely in the pan on a wire rack, then remove from the pan.

To make the icing, in a bowl, using the electric mixer, beat together the butter, confectioners' sugar, and salt on medium speed until smooth and fluffy, 2–3 minutes. Add the rose water, vanilla, and food coloring and beat until evenly colored.

Spoon the icing into a pastry bag fitted with a small star tip. Pipe the icing onto the top of each cupcake. If desired, sprinkle with the pistachios, then serve.

CHAPTER 4

Morning Treats

Merida Bear Claws

After eating the witch's Spell Cake, Merida's mother, Queen Elinor, turns into a bear. If she and Merida don't find a way to break the spell by the second sunrise, Elinor is in danger of remaining a bear forever. These bear claws, which are easy to make with purchased puff pastry, conceal a sweet spiced almond filling that stays extra moist from the addition of cake crumbs. For the crumbs, crumble an unfrosted vanilla cupcake. Or change up the flavor with chocolate cake crumbs!

3½ oz almond paste, grated

½ cup almond flour

¼ cup sugar

½ teaspoon ground cinnamon

¼ teaspoon salt

½ cup vanilla cake crumbs

Grated zest of 1 lemon

1 large egg

1 teaspoon pure vanilla extract

All-purpose flour for the work surface

1 package (about 1 lb) frozen puff pastry (2 sheets), thawed according to package directions

1 large egg beaten with 1 teaspoon water for brushing

About ¼ cup sliced almonds

Confectioners' sugar for dusting

Makes 8 bear claws

In a food processor, combine the almond paste, almond flour, sugar, cinnamon, and salt and process until the mixture is well combined and looks like bread crumbs, about 30 seconds. Add the cake crumbs, lemon zest, egg, and vanilla and process until the mixture is well combined and clumps together, about 30 seconds. Transfer to a bowl, cover, and refrigerate until the mixture is well chilled, about 1 hour.

Line 2 rimmed baking sheets with parchment paper. Lightly flour a work surface with all-purpose flour and lay a puff pastry sheet on it. Using a lightly floured rolling pin, roll out the sheet into a 10- to 11-inch square ⅛ inch thick. Cut the sheet into 4 equal squares and transfer to a prepared pan. Repeat with the second sheet and transfer to the same pan. If not shaping the pastries right away, refrigerate the squares until ready to shape.

Line up the pastry squares side by side on a clean work surface. Brush the bottom halves of the pastry squares with egg wash. Spoon about 2 tablespoonfuls of the filling onto the center of each square, then form the filling into a horizontal log, leaving about a ½-inch border on each end. For each pastry, fold the top half of the pastry over the log so the top and bottom edges line up, then press down on the sides to encase the filling. Using a paring knife, cut 4 evenly spaced slits, each about 1 inch long, along the bottom edge to create 5 strips. Separate the strips by curving the pastry into a crescent shape, then transfer the pastry to a prepared pan. Repeat to shape the remaining pastries, dividing them equally between the prepared pans.

Brush the pastries with the remaining egg wash and then sprinkle them evenly with the almonds. Bake until puffed and golden brown, 20–25 minutes. Transfer the pastries to wire racks and let cool completely. Using a fine-mesh sieve, dust with confectioners' sugar before serving.

Cinderella's Magical Pumpkin Bread

Pumpkin spice bread makes for a magical breakfast and can easily be conjured up whether you are Cinderella's Fairy Godmother or not. The secret to this bread is the addition of apple cider, which adds an extra boost of autumn spices. This recipe makes two standard-size loaves, one to keep and one to give away or put into the freezer for another time. It also makes a terrific midnight snack!

Unsalted butter for the pans

3½ cups all-purpose flour

2 teaspoons baking soda

1½ tablespoons pumpkin pie spice

1 teaspoon salt

4 large eggs

1½ cups granulated sugar

1 cup firmly packed light brown sugar

1 cup canola oil

⅔ cup apple cider

1 can (15 oz) pumpkin purée (about 1½ cups)

½ cup chopped pecans or walnuts, lightly toasted (optional)

Makes 2 loaves

Preheat the oven to 350°F. Generously butter two 9 x 5 x 3-inch loaf pans or two 6-cup molded pumpkin pans.

In a medium bowl, sift together the flour, baking soda, pumpkin pie spice, and salt. In a large bowl, whisk together the eggs and the granulated and brown sugars. Add the oil, cider, and pumpkin and whisk to combine. Add flour mixture and nuts to the pumpkin mixture and stir just until fully moistened and the nuts are evenly distributed.

Divide the batter evenly between the prepared pans. Bake the breads until richly golden brown and a toothpick inserted into the center of a loaf comes out clean, about 50 minutes for the 9 x 5-inch pans and 1 hour 10 minutes for the 6-cup pans. Let cool in the pans on wire racks for a few minutes, then turn the loaves out onto the wire racks and let cool completely. The loaves can be well wrapped and stored at room temperature for up to 7 days.

Recipe Twist

A spoonful of unsweetened applesauce is a nutritious partner that brings out the spices in the bread without overpowering the pumpkin flavor.

Aladdin Cave of Wonders' Forbidden Treasure

Protected by a tiger-shaped sand guardian, the Cave of Wonders is a secret cavern filled with treasures and magical artifacts, including the Genie's magic lamp. The cave can be entered only by someone who is worthy on the inside and has nothing to gain from the cave's riches. These gluten-free baked apples are filled with a nutty granola "treasure" and topped with a sweet honey-apple syrup.

¼ cup dried currants

1 cup apple cider

4 crisp-tart baking apples, such as Gala, Honeycrisp, or Pink Lady

1 cup oat-based granola

¼ cup chopped almonds or pecans, toasted

¼ cup apple juice concentrate

⅓ cup honey

Makes 4 servings

Put the currants into a small heatproof bowl. In a small saucepan over high heat, bring the cider to a boil. Remove from the heat, pour over the currants, and let stand until the currants have plumped, about 30 minutes.

Preheat the oven to 350°F. Cut a ½-inch-thick slice off the stem end of each apple. Using a melon baller, scoop out the core from each apple, being careful not to puncture the base of the apple. Then, carve out the flesh to leave a shell ½ inch thick. Stand the apples upright in a baking dish just large enough to hold them.

Drain the plumped currants into a fine-mesh sieve held over the baking dish. In a bowl, stir together the granola, almonds, and currants. Spoon the granola mixture into the apple cavities, heaping it high. Cut out four 5-inch squares of aluminum foil and tent a foil square over the stuffing in each apple.

Bake the apples until a knife pierces the bottom with only slight resistance, but the sides retain their shape, 35–40 minutes. Remove from the oven and lift off the foil. Let the apples cool in the dish for about 20 minutes, then transfer to a platter. Spoon any of the stuffing that fell off back in place. Discard the liquid in the dish.

In a saucepan over medium-high heat, bring the apple juice concentrate and honey to a boil. Reduce the heat to medium and simmer until the liquid is syrupy and reduced by about one-third, about 8 minutes. Spoon the hot glaze over the stuffing and apples. Serve warm or at room temperature.

Tiana's New Orleans Beignets

Tiana, an accomplished chef, dreams of owning her own restaurant. In order to get enough money to purchase an old sugar mill that she hopes to convert into a restaurant, she makes beignets for a masquerade ball being held in Naveen's honor. Grown-ups will want to accompany these pillowy pastries with New Orleans–style chicory coffee, while kids may prefer hot chocolate.

1 package (2½ teaspoons) active dry yeast

¼ cup warm water (110°F)

4½ cups all-purpose flour, plus more for the work surface

3 tablespoons granulated sugar

1 teaspoon salt

1 cup whole milk

4 tablespoons (½ stick) unsalted butter

1 large egg

Peanut or canola oil for deep-frying

Confectioners' sugar for dusting

Makes about 12 beignets

In a small bowl, sprinkle the yeast over the warm water and let stand until a creamy foam forms, 5–10 minutes. In a food processor, combine 3 cups of the flour, the granulated sugar, and salt and process briefly to mix.

In a small saucepan over medium heat, combine the milk and butter and heat gently until the milk is warm but not steaming and the butter melts. Remove from the heat. With the processor running, pour the milk mixture through the feed tube and process until blended. Add the egg, yeast mixture, and the remaining 1½ cups flour and process just until a soft dough forms. Oil a large bowl, transfer the dough to it, cover the bowl with plastic wrap, and let the dough rise in a warm, draft-free spot until doubled in size, about 1 hour.

Preheat the oven to 200°F. Line a rimmed baking sheet with paper towels. Pour oil to a depth of 3 inches into a deep, heavy saucepan and heat to 360°F on a deep-frying thermometer.

While the oil is heating, divide the dough in half. On a lightly floured surface, roll out one half of the dough into a rectangle about ¼ inch thick. Cut into 6 equal rectangles.

When the oil is ready, drop 2 or 3 rectangles into the oil and fry, turning once, until puffed and brown, about 2 minutes on each side. Using a wire skimmer or slotted spoon, transfer to the towel-lined baking sheet and keep warm in the oven. Repeat with the remaining rectangles and then with the remaining dough.

Arrange the beignets on a warmed plate and, using a fine-mesh sieve, dust them heavily all over with confectioners' sugar. Serve at once.

Mulan Great Stone Dragon Buns

The Fa family's ancestors serve as the protectors of Mulan's family and include guardians in the form of Chinese zodiac animals, such as Mulan's companion Mushu the dragon who is sent to wake up the Great Stone Dragon. They are awakened when Mulan decides to join the army in order to protect her elderly father from having to enlist. These classic stuffed baked buns, which are found in many Chinese bakeries, are filled with a sweet paste made from red adzuki beans. Hot from the oven, they are wonderfully light and fluffy.

For the Filling

1 cup dried adzuki beans, soaked overnight in cold water to cover and drained

6 cups water

½ cup sugar

2 tablespoons unsalted butter, at room temperature

½ teaspoon salt

For the Dough

1 cup whole milk, warmed (110°F)

⅓ cup sugar

1 tablespoon active dry yeast

4 cups all-purpose flour

2 large eggs

1 teaspoon salt

6 tablespoons (¾ stick) unsalted butter, at room temperature

Canola oil for the bowl

1 large egg beaten with 1 teaspoon water for brushing

2 teaspoons toasted sesame seeds

Makes 12 buns

To make the filling, in a saucepan over high heat, combine the beans and water and bring to a boil. Reduce the heat to medium-low and simmer, stirring every so often, until the beans are very tender and starting to break down, about 45 minutes.

Pour the beans into a fine-mesh sieve to drain. Transfer the beans to a food processor, add the sugar, butter, and salt, and process to a smooth purée, about 2 minutes. Transfer the purée to the sieve and set the sieve over a saucepan. Using a rubber spatula, press the purée through the sieve to remove the bean skins.

Place the pan over low heat and cook, stirring constantly, until the mixture is very thick, about 7 minutes. Transfer the bean mixture to a bowl, cover with a piece of plastic wrap, pressing it directly onto the surface (to prevent a crust from forming), and set aside to cool completely. (You should have about 1½ cups filling.)

To make the dough, in a stand mixer, stir together the milk, sugar, and yeast. Let stand until a creamy foam forms, 5–10 minutes. Add the flour, eggs, and salt to the yeast mixture. Attach the dough hook and knead the dough on medium-low speed until it starts to look shaggy, 3–5 minutes. While continuing to knead, add the butter a tablespoon at a time. Then continue to knead until the dough is fairly smooth and mostly pulls away from the sides of the bowl (it will be fairly sticky), about 10 minutes.

Oil a large bowl. Gather the dough into a ball, transfer it to the oiled bowl, cover the bowl with plastic wrap, and let rise in a warm, draft-free spot until doubled in size, about 1½ hours.

Continued on page 122